GREEK COOKING FOR THE GODS

Eva Zane

101 PRODUCTIONS

To my mother and father, Anna and George

Publisher	Brete C. Harrison
Associate Publisher	James Connolly
Editors	Annette Gooch and Carolyn Chandler
Interior Designers	Linda Hauck and Charlene Mouille
Director of Production	Steve Lux

Note: There is no standard transliteration system for the Greek language. The spellings used in this book are those most commonly found in Greek culinary works that have been transcribed in the Roman alphabet. This book also uses many Greek and Greek-American colloquial terms and phrases.

"Hestia, Keeper of the Hearth" by Homer. *The Oxford: Book of Greek Verse in Translation*, Ed. T.F. Higham and C.M. Bowra. London: The Clarendon Press, 1938. Reprinted with permission.

Cover Design by Glenn Martinez and Associates
Cover photography by Kevin Sanchez
Food stylist: Susan Massey-Weil
Photographic stylist: Liz Ross
Photographer's assistant: Chris Coughlin
Illustrations by W. Busser Howell

Distributed to the book trade by Publishers Group West and to gift/gourmet trade by Max Burton Enterprises, Inc.

Printed and bound in the USA
Published by 101 Productions/The Cole Group
4415 Sonoma Highway, PO Box 4089
Santa Rosa, CA 95402-4089

A B C D E F G H
2 3 4 5 6 7 8 9

Library of Congress Catalog Card Number in progress
ISBN 1-56426-501-3

GREEK COOKING FOR THE GODS

Introduction 5

1 Dionysus and the Wines and Appetizers of Greece 9

> Wines and Apéritifs 10
> Greek Cheeses 13
> Filo Dough 14
> Appetizers 15

2 Demeter and the Foods from the Earth 31

> Soups 32
> Salads 40
> Vegetable Entrées and Side Dishes 47
> Rice and Noodles 66
> Sweets and Breads 73

3 Poseidon and the Foods from the Sea 93

> Fish and Shrimp 94
> Salt Cod, Octopus, Squid, and Eel 107

4 Pan and the Foods from the Flocks 115

> Kid and Lamb 116
> Veal, Beef, and Pork 138

5 Artemis and the Foods from the Hunt 149

> Game Birds, Rabbit, and Venison 150
> Turkey, Goose, Duck, Squab, and Chicken 156

6 Hestia and the Basics of Greek Cooking 171

> Sauces, Dressings, and Yogurt 172

Menus for Special Occasions 183

Index 187

ABOUT THE AUTHOR

*B*orn in New England of Greek parents, Eva Zane has spent a lifetime absorbing and studying the culinary and cultural traditions of her beloved Greece. Although her parents were actors by profession, both shared a profound knowledge and love of Greek cooking. Young Evoula Stamatoginnis, as she was then known, was an eager pupil. Her earliest memories in Boston, and later Chicago, center around her culinary heritage: watching her father prepare the traditional Easter kid and visiting the ethnic markets of Halsted Street with her mother to select the seafood for fish soup. Both Eva and her sister married restaurateurs, and much of her adult life, consequently, has been involved with food. She herself has also operated several restaurants of Greek and Middle Eastern cuisine in San Francisco. In this book, she brings to you both the classic and modern dishes of the Aegean isles, as well as some innovative dishes from her own and her parents' kitchens.

INTRODUCTION

Although few would dispute the artistic and intellectual attainments of Greek civilization, the many contributions of the Greek kitchen to the world's cuisines have been largely ignored. Indeed, centuries before the birth of Christ, when the rest of Europe was surviving on little more than haunches of raw meat, the Greeks were dining on legumes simmered with olive oil, oregano, and bay; grape leaves stuffed with chopped spiced meat; lamb roasted with capers; and honey-drenched cakes.

Much of what we know about the cookery of ancient Greece comes down to us from a second-century A.D. work titled *The Deipnosophists* ("The Banquet of the Learned"), written when Greece was under the rule of the Romans. Its author, Athenaeus, a native of Egypt who resided in Rome, includes a provocative picture of the Greek culinary landscape—its banquets, dining etiquette, conversations, kitchen routines. He talks of Homer, Herodotus, and Sophocles and their interests in the origins and healthfulness of a host of foods.

Over the centuries, the Greeks combined their sophisticated traditions with the food customs of neighbors, traders, and invaders. They adopted paper-thin filo pastry and fruits preserved in syrup from Persia; rice, lemons, and eggplants from India; and thick, strong coffee and skewered meats from the Turks, who ruled the Greeks for four centuries.

The Greeks were also great exporters of culinary ideas. Bouillabaisse, considered by many to be a French classic, was actually introduced to Marseilles by Greek seafarers. Neither is béchamel sauce a Gallic original; Athenaeus credits a Greek named Orion with its invention. Mayonnaise commonly appeared on menus during the Hellenistic age. The first gingerbread was baked on Rhodes, and the Greeks were fattening fowls for the table centuries before the Romans did. The olive, grape, and fig all flourished in ancient Greece.

Thus, Greek cuisine, like Greece itself, has a long and honorable history. I want to share with you both the classic and the modern dishes of my ancestral homeland, plus some creative innovations from my own and my parents' kitchens. The result is a volume of Greek cookery that is truly fit for the gods.

Shall we now, together,
tread upon ground where gods dwelled
and share their fare?
On to Mount Olympus, philhellenes!
To feast and discourse with the gods.

Dionysus, The God of Wine

Dionysus, Olympian in stature,
unlike your Roman counterpart, Bacchus.
Yours is a solemn cult,
of which tragedy was born,
the name derived from
the sacrifice of goats,
accompanied by song and dance.
Tragedy, tragoidia, goat song.
Dionysus, giver of nectar,
in your name, retsina flows
like silken ribbons
upon the immortal steps of Plaka.

DIONYSUS AND THE WINES AND APPETIZERS OF GREECE

Wines and Apéritifs

*D*espite a long history of wine consumption, Greeks did not and most still do not drink their wine full strength. They prefer it diluted with water, in accordance with the motto *pan metro arasto*, "nothing to excess." Greeks will also not drink without eating, so when serving Greek wine or ouzo as an apéritif, accompany it with an assortment of appetizers (see pages 15 to 29).

Wine followed olive oil as the main export of ancient Greece. From the sixth century B.C. until the first century B.C., Greece produced the finest wines in the Mediterranean; the vintages of Chios and Lesbos were particularly admired.

The best-known of the Greek wines is retsina, which is flavored with pine resin. There are many legends as to its origin, but I have a favorite: The Athenians, in an attempt to save their wine from being drunk by the invading Persians, decided to make it distasteful by adding pine resin to it. The Persians found the mixture undrinkable, but when the Greeks reopened the jars, they were delighted with the flavor. They have been drinking resinated wine ever since.

A less romantic legend has the Greeks fermenting and storing their wines in jars and goatskins coated with resin. Having soon acquired a taste for the resinated wine they added bags filled with aromatic gums to "improve" the flavor still further.

The ancient Greeks, even in the most marginal times, served an apéritif called *propoma*, a wine flavored with herbs and spices. At the end of the day they would gather together *(sym)* for a drink *(posis)* and intellectual discussion. Thus was born the word *symposium.*

There are many Greek wines, brandies, and liqueurs available in North American markets. Descriptions of some of the most popular follow. Greeks tend to drink the wines that appeal to them; they do not follow strict customs with regard to which wines should be drunk with certain foods. You should do the same.

Red and Rosé Wines

The red wines should be served at room temperature; the rosés taste best when slightly chilled.

NEMEA—A dry, red wine from a town of the same name.

OTHELLO—Dry, full-bodied wine from Cyprus.

PENDELI—Dry, light table wines from vineyards near Athens.

RODITYS—A dry rosé made from the grape of the same name; very popular.

White Wines

In general, white wines are served well chilled, but the more delicate vintages are poured slightly chilled.

DEMESTICA—Dry and very light.

HYMETTUS—Dry, full flavor; named for a famous mountain near Athens.

ROBOLA—Dry and full-bodied; from the island of Samos.

ST. HELENA—Highly regarded and very dry.

ST. PANTELEIMON AND APHRODITE—Highly regarded dry wines from Cyprus.

Resinated Wines

Resinated white wines are usually drunk well chilled. The rosés should be drunk slightly chilled.

FILERI—White retsina from Arcadia.

KOKINELI—A lightly resinated rosé.

RETSINA—Dry, resinated white.

Apéritifs, Sweet Wines, Liqueurs, and Brandies

The sweet wines, which are commonly offered after a meal, are served at room temperature, as are these other generally sweet beverages.

FOKKIOS—Sweet after-dinner wine from Macedonia.

MASTICHA—Apéritif flavored with sap of mastic tree; clear but turns milky when mixed with water.

MAVRODAPHNE—An all-purpose sweet red wine; grown near the port of Patras.

METAXA—A full-bodied brandy.

MUSCAT—Sweet fortified dessert wine; the most famous muscat-grape wine comes from the island of Samos and was a favorite of Lord Byron.

NIKA—A sherry from Cyprus.

OUZO—An anise-flavored liqueur; clear but turns milky when mixed with water.

Greek Cheeses

The harsh terrain of Greece restricts livestock to the tenacious sheep and goat. Cheese production is therefore dependent upon what can be made from the milks of these animals. Despite this seeming limitation, the Greeks are great cheese eaters, registering one of the highest per capita consumption rates in the world. In fact, domestic demand for cheese is so great that little is exported.

Greek-style cheeses, however, are manufactured on a large scale in Cyprus, Denmark, Australia, Canada, and the United States. Sadly, the Greeks, unable to meet domestic needs, now find themselves in the position of having to import their most famous cheese, feta, from other countries.

Feta is a salty, crumbly cheese traditionally made from sheep's milk or goat's milk. In Denmark, Germany, Australia, and North America feta is often made from cow's milk. It is both a table cheese and a cooking cheese and is readily available in well-stocked supermarkets.

Kefalotyri, which is often called for in this book, is made from sheep's milk; it has a slightly oily quality and is mainly a grating cheese. Italian Parmesan is a satisfactory substitute.

Kasseri is a soft, mild sheep's or goat's milk cheese similar to Italian mozzarella. It can be sliced and fried or eaten as a table cheese. *Mizithra* is available as a fresh cheese reminiscent of Italian ricotta, as a salted cheese, and also as an aged cheese for grating.

Other popular cheeses include *graviera,* a yellow, sheep's milk table cheese, and *manouri,* a very creamy cheese from Crete sometimes eaten with honey as a dessert.

Filo Dough

*M*ade from a wheat-flour dough, filo comes in paper-thin sheets, which are sold in slender 1-pound boxes in specialty food shops and well-stocked supermarkets. A box contains about 24 sheets, although some brands contain only 16 to 20 sheets. The sheets also vary in size. Some measure 16 by 18 inches, others measure 14 by 18 inches, and still others measure only 9 by 13 inches. Most areas of the country carry only one brand of filo; all of these sizes, however, will work for the recipes in this book. If you have a choice of brands, thinner sheets (greater number of sheets per pound) measuring 14 by 18 inches are preferred.

Many shops keep filo in the freezer compartment rather than the cold case. If you purchase it frozen, defrost it in the refrigerator overnight. Do not attempt to refreeze it. Fresh filo must be refrigerated; if unopened, it will keep up to 1 month. Once opened, it should be used within 1 week.

Before beginning to work with filo, remove it from the refrigerator and bring to room temperature; do not unwrap it, however, until you are going to use it. Ready all of the other ingredients, then remove filo from box. Slip off plastic inner wrapper and unroll filo on a large, flat work surface. Cover stack of filo sheets with a sheet of waxed paper topped with a lightly dampened tea towel. This is important, because if the filo dries out it will crack and be very difficult to handle.

Uncover only as many sheets as you will be working with at one time. Most recipes direct you to brush the sheets with butter; be liberal about the amount you use, since this keeps the filo from crumbling. It is also important to work as quickly as possible.

Appetizers

GGGGGGGGGGGGGGGGGGGGGGGGGGGGGGGGGGGGGGGGGGGGGGGGGGGGGGGGGGGGGGGGGGGGGGGGGGGGGGGGG

Whether in the countryside or the city, the custom is the same: The Greek always extends a hand in hospitality to a visitor. In fact, the Greek word *xenos* means both "guest" and "foreigner." Even in the most remote villages, a newcomer is welcomed with a slice of goat's milk cheese and a wedge of bread hot from an outdoor oven. Often there will be cucumbers and the fish roe purée known as *taramosalata*. If you are near the sea, fish, perhaps whitebait *(marides)* caught that morning, will be cooked over a hot fire in a fruity olive oil, then splashed with juice from a just-picked lemon.

In the cities, when twilight invades the sky, Greeks head for the tavernas for an hour or so of conversation, a glass of anise-flavored ouzo or chilled retsina, and an assortment of *mezadakia* ("appetizers"). Small plates hold olives, marinated mushrooms, rice-stuffed grape leaves, and crisp pastry triangles filled with spinach and feta—foods designed to whet the appetite for the meal to follow.

Stuffed Grape Leaves
Dolmadakia

Greeks love to celebrate special occasions of every kind, from wedding ceremonies to religious feast days. A platter of stuffed grape leaves is an indispensable dish on any festive menu. If you have access to pesticide-free grapevines, gather fresh, young leaves; immerse them in hot water until pliable; cool; and fill as directed here. Otherwise, buy grape leaves bottled in brine from a Greek grocery or a well-stocked supermarket.

¼ cup dried currants
1 cup dry white wine
12 tablespoons olive oil
6 green onions (including some green
*   top), finely chopped*
1 tablespoon minced fresh parsley
¾ cup long-grain white rice
1 tablespoon minced fresh dill
¼ cup pine nuts
Salt and freshly ground pepper, to taste
1 jar (16 oz) grape leaves preserved in
*   brine*
Boiling water
Juice of 2 lemons
2 cups beef stock
Lemon wedges and chilled plain yogurt,
*   for accompaniment*

In a small bowl combine currants and wine; set aside. In a small skillet over medium heat, warm 2 tablespoons of the oil. Add onions and parsley and sauté until onions are translucent (about 5 minutes). Add rice, dill, pine nuts, currants and wine, salt, and pepper; stir to mix, cover, and simmer until liquid is absorbed (about 10 minutes). Remove from heat and cool.

Remove grape leaves from jar and immerse in boiling water about 30 seconds; drain and rinse under cold water. Cut off and discard tough stems. Pat leaves dry with paper towels, then place shiny side down on a flat surface.

Place a rounded teaspoon of the rice mixture on center of each leaf. Fold base end of leaf over filling to cover; fold in sides of leaf, overlapping them, then roll up carefully to form a sealed cylinder about 2 inches long. Repeat with remaining leaves.

In bottom of a dutch oven or other heavy, broad-bottomed pan, arrange a layer of stuffed leaves, seam side down, close together. Sprinkle with some of the lemon juice and 2 tablespoons of the olive oil. Repeat, making as many layers as necessary to accommodate all of the stuffed leaves; sprinkle each layer with lemon juice and 2 tablespoons olive oil. Pour in beef stock and the remaining olive oil, being careful not to disturb layers.

Place a heavy plate on top to weight down stuffed leaves. Cover and simmer over very low heat until rice is tender (about 40 minutes). To test, open one of the packets.

Remove from heat and lift stuffed leaves out with a slotted utensil. Arrange on a platter and cool completely. Serve with lemon wedges and yogurt.

Makes about 3 dozen stuffed leaves

Feta Cheese Triangles

Tiropetes

Read the information on handling filo dough (see page 14) before beginning to assemble these rich, flaky triangles. The recipe yields about eight dozen pastries, so freeze some of them unbaked for a future gathering. They can go directly from the freezer to the oven.

1 cup Basic White Sauce (see page 174)
1 pound feta cheese, crumbled
1 cup freshly grated kefalotyri or
*   Parmesan cheese*
3 eggs, lightly beaten
2 tablespoons minced fresh parsley
1 cup butter, melted and cooled
1 pound filo dough, thawed overnight in
*   refrigerator if frozen*

Prepare white sauce; transfer to a mixing bowl and set aside to cool to room temperature.

Preheat oven to 375° F. Add cheeses, eggs, parsley, and 3 tablespoons of the butter to cooled sauce; mix well.

Place filo dough on a flat work surface. Cut sheets lengthwise in strips 3 inches wide and about 12 inches long. Work with 2 or 3 strips at a time, keeping others covered so they don't dry out. Brush strips with melted butter and place about 1 teaspoon of the cheese mixture about ½ inch in from base of strip. Fold the base end over to cover the filling as you would fold a flag, forming a triangular shape; bottom of strip should now align with left side of strip. Then bring bottom point of strip straight up along left side. Fold again on

diagonal, this time so left side meets right side. Continue folding in this "flag fashion" until you reach the end of the strip. You will have an enclosed triangular packet. Repeat with remaining strips and filling.

Arrange triangles on baking sheets and brush tops with melted butter. Bake until golden (15 to 20 minutes). Serve at once.

Makes about 8 dozen triangles

WBH

Meat Triangles
Kreatopetes

᎒᎒᎒᎒᎒᎒᎒᎒᎒᎒᎒᎒᎒᎒᎒᎒᎒᎒᎒᎒᎒᎒᎒᎒᎒᎒᎒᎒᎒᎒

A mixture of ground beef, grated cheese, and minced hard-cooked egg fills these pastries. If you have fresh filo dough on hand, this recipe, which yields only two dozen triangles, can be put together quickly for serving unexpected guests.

¼ pound lean ground beef
2 tablespoons freshly grated kefalotyri or
*   Parmesan cheese*
1 hard-cooked egg, minced
8 sheets filo dough, thawed overnight in
*   refrigerator if frozen*
⅓ cup butter, melted and cooled

Preheat oven to 375° F. In a small dry skillet over medium-high heat, sauté beef until browned (6 to 8 minutes). In a mixing bowl combine beef, cheese, and egg; mix well.

Following directions for Feta Cheese Triangles (see page 17), form triangles, using filo, butter, and beef filling, then bake as directed.

Makes about 2 dozen triangles

Shellfish Triangles
Psaropetes

᎒᎒᎒᎒᎒᎒᎒᎒᎒᎒᎒᎒᎒᎒᎒᎒᎒᎒᎒᎒᎒᎒᎒᎒᎒᎒᎒᎒᎒᎒᎒᎒᎒

*T*hese shellfish-stuffed pastries are an excellent first course for an elegant dinner.

½ cup each cooked shrimp and flaked
*   cooked crabmeat*
½ cup Basic White Sauce (see page 174)
1 tablespoon minced fresh parsley
Dash freshly squeezed lemon juice
8 sheets filo dough, thawed overnight in
*   refrigerator if frozen*
⅓ cup butter, melted and cooled

Preheat oven to 375° F. In a mixing bowl combine shellfish, white sauce, parsley, and lemon juice; mix well.

Following directions for Feta Cheese Triangles (see page 17), form triangles, using filo, butter, and shellfish filling; then bake as directed.

Makes about 2 dozen triangles

Spinach-Cheese Triangles
Spanakopetes

Here I have used the filling for our classic *spanakopeta* to stuff filo triangles. Be sure to dry the spinach very well before mixing it with the other ingredients; excess moisture will cause the pastry to become soggy.

> *2 cups filling for Spinach-Cheese Pie*
> *(see page 49)*
> *10 to 12 sheets filo dough, thawed*
> *overnight in refrigerator if frozen*
> *½ cup butter, melted and cooled*

Preheat oven to 375° F. Prepare filling. Following directions for Feta Cheese Triangles (see page 17), form triangles, using filo, butter, and spinach-cheese filling, then bake as directed.

Makes about 3 dozen triangles

Fried Cheese
Kasseri Tiganismeno

This simple dish is usually prepared with *kasseri* cheese, which is made from sheep's milk. Look for kasseri in Greek delicatessens and in specialty cheese shops. Accompany these rich squares with ouzo or your favorite apéritif.

> *4 ounces kasseri cheese*
> *¼ cup olive oil or butter*
> *Juice of ½ lemon*

Cut cheese in ¼-inch-thick slices, then cut in 1-inch squares. In a heavy skillet over medium-high heat, warm oil. When oil is hot, slip cheese squares into the pan and fry, turning once, until golden on both sides. Transfer to a warmed platter, drizzle lemon juice over the top, and serve at once.

Serves 4

Cucumbers Stuffed with Feta
Angouria Yemista me Feta

ьг

*T*he Worcestershire sauce in this cheese filling is a Greek-American addition; it contributes a bit of sharpness to the already tangy feta. Serve the stuffed cucumber halves on individual plates as a first course, or cut in bite-sized pieces and offer as part of a *mezadakia* platter. Allow time to chill the stuffed cucumbers thoroughly before serving.

½ cup crumbled feta cheese
1 tablespoon mayonnaise
2 drops Worcestershire sauce
4 small cucumbers, chilled
1 tablespoon minced fresh parsley, for
garnish

In a small bowl combine cheese, mayonnaise, and Worcestershire sauce; mix well.

Peel cucumbers and cut in half lengthwise. With a small spoon scoop out seeds from each half, forming a shallow trough the length of the cucumber.

Fill cucumber halves with cheese mixture. Chill well; garnish with parsley just before serving.

Serves 4 as a first course
or 8 with other hors d'oeuvres

Broiled Tomatoes with Feta
Domates me Feta

гьг

*B*roiled tomatoes are a superb first course before an entrée of roasted meat or poultry, or they may be used as a garnish on almost any dinner plate. Cut tomatoes in half in a zigzag pattern for a more attractive presentation.

4 medium-sized firm, ripe tomatoes
2 to 3 ounces feta cheese
Minced fresh or crushed dried oregano,
to taste

Preheat broiler. Cut tomatoes in half crosswise or in thick slices. Carefully remove seeds.

In a small bowl mash cheese with a fork; mix in oregano. Strew cheese mixture over cut side of tomato halves or top of slices.

Arrange on flameproof baking sheet and broil until cheese is lightly browned and tomato is heated through (5 to 8 minutes).

Serves 4 as first course or 8 as a garnish

Marinated Mushrooms

Manitaria Marinata

Arrange these fennel-infused mushrooms on a bed of chilled lettuce leaves for a first course. Select very fresh, small domestic mushrooms with tightly closed caps. This basic marinade can also be used with other vegetables, including cauliflower florets, zucchini slices, and artichoke hearts. If using one of these vegetables, adjust simmering time so that the vegetable cooks until just tender. Note that this dish needs to chill before serving.

½ cup olive oil
⅓ cup freshly squeezed lemon juice
1 sprig thyme or ½ teaspoon dried thyme,
*   crushed*
Feathery tops from 1 stalk fennel or
*   ¼ teaspoon fennel seed*
1 clove garlic, finely slivered
1 stalk celery, minced
10 black peppercorns
1 bay leaf
½ cup water
2 pounds fresh button mushrooms
1 lemon
2 tablespoons minced fresh parsley, for
*   garnish*

In a saucepan combine oil, lemon juice, thyme, fennel, garlic, celery, peppercorns, bay leaf, and the water. Bring to a boil, cover, reduce heat, and simmer until celery is just tender (about 5 minutes).

Meanwhile, trim off mushroom stems. Cut lemon in half and rub mushroom caps with cut sides of lemon. Add caps to simmering liquid and cook 5 minutes. Remove mushrooms with a slotted utensil and arrange on a serving dish.

Raise heat and boil liquid until it reduces and thickens. Pour sauce over mushrooms, cool, cover, and chill well. Just before serving garnish with parsley.

Serves 6 as a first course
or 8 to 10 with other hors d'oeuvres

Fish Roe Purée
Taramosalata

*M*ost Greeks regard *taramosalata* as the most delectable of all appetizers. Firm, pale pink *tarama* (salted fish roe) forms the basis of the rich purée, here offered as a dip with crackers. The purée also can be spread on toast points and garnished with minced hard-cooked eggs, or mounded in cucumber shells or fluted tomato halves and used to garnish whole baked fish or roasted meats. Avocado with Fish Roe Purée (see page 45) showcases the creamy roe in a salad.

Tarama can be purchased in jars in Greek groceries. Be sure to buy pure salted fish roe; avoid products that contain other substances or food coloring. Mullet roe has the best flavor and consistency for this dish but is extremely rare; salted carp or cod roe may be used instead.

7 slices white bread, preferably from a
*   European-style loaf*
1 jar (7 oz) tarama
2 tablespoons grated onion
Juice of 2 lemons
¾ cup olive oil
Minced fresh parsley and Kalamata
*   olives, for garnish*
Crackers, for accompaniment

Lightly toast bread slices, then trim off and discard crusts. Soak bread in water to cover; drain and squeeze out all moisture. Set aside.

In a food processor or blender, slowly process tarama until creamy. Add onion, bread, and lemon juice and blend until smooth. With machine running, add oil in a fine, steady stream, blending until mixture is light in color and very creamy.

To serve, mound purée in a bowl and garnish with parsley and a few olives. Accompany with crackers.

Makes about 4 cups
Serves 12 or more with other hors d'oeuvres

Fried Whitebait

Marides Tighanites

Crisply fried small fish, simply dressed with fresh lemon juice, are a must for a *mezadakia*. *Whitebait* is the British term for various varieties of tiny fish pulled from European waters. North American markets carry small white fish called *smelts*, which are a good substitute.

Look for smelts no more than about four inches long. The heads and tails should be left intact; true smelt aficionados savor the whole fish. These delicate fried fish are also sometimes served with a currant sauce.

> *2½ to 3 pounds smelts, cleaned*
> *Flour, as needed*
> *Olive oil, for frying*
> *1 clove garlic, minced*
> *½ cup dry white wine (optional)*
> *Juice of 2 lemons*
> *Lemon wedges, for accompaniment*

Rinse smelts in cold water; pat dry with paper towels.

Spread flour on a flat plate. In a large, heavy skillet over high heat, pour oil to a depth of about ¼ inch. Heat until a light haze forms on the surface. Add garlic and cook briefly until fragrant. Dredge fish in flour, shake off excess, and slip fish into oil. Brown on both sides, turning once, until crisp and golden (2 to 3 minutes). Do not crowd pan or oil temperature will drop and fish will absorb too much oil. If desired, add wine to pan, then move pan rapidly back and forth over burner a few moments so fish will absorb wine.

With a slotted utensil transfer fish to paper towels to drain briefly. Remove to a platter and drizzle with lemon juice. Fry remaining fish in same manner. Serve immediately or at room temperature; accompany with lemon wedges.

Serves 10 to 12 with other hors d'oeuvres

Shrimp in Their Shells, Plaka Style
Garides à la Plaka

The Plaka, a neighborhood of twisting, stone-paved streets at the base of the Acropolis, once housed the elite of Athens. Today it is filled with bouzouki clubs reverberating with Zorba music and with little tavernas serving these garlicky shrimp.

Unpeeled shrimp may at first seem like too much work to eat, but your reward is the taste of the sea bursting in your mouth when you bite into them. Accompany these succulent shellfish with a chilled white wine and plenty of crusty bread for dunking in the sauce.

2 pounds medium-large unpeeled shrimp
4 cloves garlic, minced
1 cup minced fresh parsley
Juice of 3 lemons
3 tablespoons minced fresh oregano
1 cup olive oil
1 cup dry sherry
Salt and freshly ground pepper, to taste
Lemon wedges, for accompaniment

Preheat oven to 450° F. Place shrimp in a roasting pan. Combine remaining ingredients, except lemon wedges, and pour over shrimp. Mix well to coat shrimp thoroughly.

Bake shrimp until they turn pink (10 to 15 minutes). Transfer to a heated serving platter, pour pan juices over the top, and surround with lemon wedges.

Serves 6

24

Pickled Squid

Kalamaria Toursi

*I*f you prefer, enclose the pickling spice in a cheesecloth bag and remove the bag before the dish is served. The Greek custom, however, is to add the spices loose. Note that the squid must be marinated overnight.

> *3 pounds squid*
> *1 cup bottled clam juice*
> *1 cup water*
> *½ cup olive oil*
> *1 cup distilled white vinegar*
> *3 cloves garlic, slivered*
> *2½ teaspoons mixed whole pickling spice*
> *½ cup white retsina wine*
> *2 teaspoons dried oregano, crushed*
> *Salt and freshly ground pepper, to taste*
> *1 lemon, sliced thinly*
> *Finely minced fresh parsley, lemon*
> *   wedges, and Kalamata olives, for*
> *   garnish*

Rinse squid under cold water. Gently pull on head portion; entrails will slide free from body. Place head portion on cutting board and cut off tentacles just above eyes. Remove and discard hard beak from base of tentacles and set tentacles aside; discard head and entrails. Pull transparent quill from body and discard. Rinse body inside and out. Peel off mottled skin from body and fins.

In a saucepan combine squid bodies and tentacles, clam juice, and the water. Bring to a boil, cover, reduce heat, and simmer until squid is very tender (about 35 minutes). Drain through sieve placed over bowl; reserve liquid. Cut squid bodies crosswise in ¾-inch-wide rings; leave tentacles whole.

In a deep skillet over high heat, combine squid, reserved cooking liquid, oil, vinegar, garlic, pickling spice, wine, oregano, salt, and pepper. Cover, quickly bring to a boil, reduce heat, and simmer 10 minutes.

Pour contents of skillet into a bowl, add lemon slices, cover, and chill overnight. Serve squid and marinade in a bowl or deep platter. Sprinkle with parsley and garnish with lemon wedges topped with olives.

Serves 10 to 12 with other hors d'oeuvres

Rice-Stuffed Squid
Kalamaria Yemista

For this dish you will need small, uniform-sized squid about four inches in length. Use sturdy wooden toothpicks to close tops securely.

2 pounds small squid
¾ cup olive oil
6 green onions (including some green top), chopped
1 clove garlic, minced
1 tablespoon chopped fresh parsley
½ cup long-grain white rice
¼ teaspoon dried oregano, crushed
½ cup dry sherry
1 cup finely chopped spinach
Salt and freshly ground pepper, to taste
Juice of 1 lemon
½ cup bottled clam juice
1 cup warm water
Lemon wedges, for garnish

Clean squid as directed for Pickled Squid (see page 25). Leave bodies whole and chop tentacles; reserve.

In a large, heavy skillet over medium heat, warm ¼ cup of the oil. Add onions, garlic, and parsley; sauté until mixture is lightly browned (about 8 minutes). Add rice and stir 2 minutes. Mix in oregano, sherry, spinach, reserved tentacles, salt, and pepper; cover and cook until rice is tender (20 minutes). Remove from heat and cool slightly.

Stuff squid bodies loosely (about three-quarters full) with rice mixture and secure with toothpicks. Arrange in a single layer in a large, heavy skillet. Add lemon juice, clam juice, the remaining oil, and the warm water. Bring to a boil, cover, reduce heat to low, and simmer gently over low heat until squid is tender (about 30 minutes).

With a slotted utensil remove squid to a plate; let cool completely. Remove toothpicks and slice carefully in ½-inch-wide rings; arrange rings on a platter. Surround with lemon wedges.

Serves 10 to 12 with other hors d'oeuvres

Pâté à la Grecque

GGGGGGGGGGGGGGGGGGGGGGGGGGGGGGGGGGGGGGGGGGGGGGGGGGGGGGGGGGGGGGGGGGGGGGGGGGGG

Greek cookery does not include a classic pâté. Indeed, the only places in Greece where you will find pâté are restaurants specializing in French cuisine. Following hours of experimenting in the kitchen, I have come up with an original Greek pâté. It is based on my mother's recipe for *loukanika* ("sausages"). First the casing went; then I added a few ingredients. Here is the result. The pâté must be refrigerated 24 hours before serving. Serve with your choice of bread—crusty, dark, or toasted.

> *½ pound each lean ground pork and*
> *   lamb*
> *1 pound calves' liver, cut in small pieces*
> *2 medium onions, chopped*
> *2 cloves garlic, chopped*
> *1 cup dry sherry*
> *1 teaspoon ground allspice*
> *3 bay leaves*
> *1 teaspoon dried fines herbes, crushed*
> *½ teaspoon dried thyme, crushed*
> *2 teaspoons dried oregano, crushed*
> *½ cup unsalted butter, softened, plus*
> *   butter for loaf pans*
> *¾ cup brandy*

In a large, heavy skillet over medium-low heat, combine all ingredients except butter and brandy. Stir to mix well, breaking up ground meat. Cover and cook over low heat 1 hour, stirring occasionally. Remove from heat and spoon off and discard any fat that has formed on the surface. Let cool.

Pass meat mixture, including bay leaves, through a meat grinder fitted with a coarse disk. Mix the ½ cup butter into mixture with a wooden spoon. Fit grinder with fine disk and pass meat mixture through again. Stir in brandy and pass mixture through fine disk a final time. The result will be a fine paste.

Butter two 5- by 9-inch loaf pans and divide meat mixture between them. Cover with plastic wrap and chill 24 hours. To unmold, loosen pâtés from pan sides with a long, thin knife blade. Invert on platters or a wooden board. With a sharp knife, cut in thin slices.

Serves 16 to 20 with other hors d'oeuvres

Fried Liver Bits
Sikotakia Tighanita

𝔾𝔾𝔾𝔾𝔾𝔾𝔾𝔾𝔾𝔾𝔾𝔾𝔾𝔾𝔾𝔾𝔾𝔾𝔾𝔾𝔾𝔾𝔾𝔾𝔾𝔾𝔾𝔾𝔾𝔾𝔾𝔾

The secret to preparing liver is to cook it very briefly over high heat. Long, slow cooking toughens and dries out this delicate variety meat.

2 pounds calves' liver
Salt and freshly ground pepper, to taste
½ cup olive oil
1 clove garlic, bruised
2 tablespoons minced fresh oregano
¼ cup dry white wine
Juice of 2 lemons
Minced fresh parsley and lemon wedges,
  for garnish

Trim liver of any visible fat and connective tissue. Pat surface dry and cut liver in 1½-inch squares. Sprinkle with salt and pepper and set aside.

In a large, heavy skillet over medium-high heat, warm oil. Add garlic and cook briefly until fragrant; discard garlic. Add liver and sauté briskly on all sides until lightly browned; do not overcook. Sprinkle oregano over liver; move pan rapidly back and forth over burner to toss liver with oregano. Pour in wine and lemon juice, cover, and immediately remove from heat; let stand several minutes for flavors to steep.

Remove liver to a platter; spoon pan juices over the top and serve at once. Sprinkle with parsley and garnish with lemon wedges.

Serves 8 to 10 with other hors d'oeuvres

Cocktail Meatballs
Keftaidakia

𝔾𝔾𝔾𝔾𝔾𝔾𝔾𝔾𝔾𝔾𝔾𝔾𝔾𝔾𝔾𝔾𝔾𝔾𝔾𝔾𝔾𝔾𝔾𝔾𝔾𝔾𝔾𝔾𝔾𝔾𝔾𝔾𝔾𝔾

These delicate meatballs, which are bound only with egg, taste best when served very hot. They may be prepared several hours in advance, refrigerated, and then slipped in the oven just as your guests arrive. Transfer them with their pan juices to a chafing dish and supply wooden cocktail picks for guests to spear the meatballs.

2 pounds lean ground lamb
1 onion, grated
1 clove garlic, minced
2 tablespoons minced fresh parsley
1 egg, lightly beaten
½ teaspoon each dried mint and
  oregano, crushed
¾ cup dry white wine
2 tablespoons olive oil, for baking pan

Preheat oven to 475° F. In a mixing bowl combine lamb, onion, garlic, parsley, egg, mint, oregano, and ¼ cup of the wine. Knead until very smooth.

Rub bottom and sides of a large baking pan with oil. Form meat mixture into walnut-sized balls and place in oiled pan. Bake until browned and cooked through (about 20 minutes).

Remove pan from oven, pour remaining wine over meatballs, and shake pan to turn meatballs in pan juices. Serve immediately.

**Makes about 4 dozen meatballs, serves 10 to 12
with other hors d'oeuvres**

Lamb Brains Marinated with Oregano

Miala Riganata

When making this dish plan on marinating the brains a few hours, so that they will fully absorb the flavor of the seasonings.

1½ pounds lamb or calf brains
1 bay leaf
1 onion, quartered
½ to ¾ cup olive oil
¼ cup white wine vinegar
Minced fresh oregano, to taste
Salt and freshly ground pepper, to taste
Chopped fresh parsley, for garnish

Rinse brains under cold water and place in a bowl. Add cold water to cover and let stand 15 minutes. Drain and peel away membrane and connective tissue. Rinse with cold water and place in a saucepan. Add water to cover, bay leaf, and onion. Bring to a boil, reduce heat, and simmer until tender when pierced with a fork (about 20 minutes); drain. Cool, cover, and chill until firm. Slice about ¼ inch thick and arrange slices on a platter.

In a bowl combine olive oil and vinegar; season to taste with oregano, salt, and pepper. Pour marinade over brains, cover, and chill at least 1 hour, or up to 4 hours. Garnish with parsley before serving.

Serves 6 as a first course

Demeter, The Goddess of Agriculture

She emerges in one's mind,
a noble and tragic vision,
for the sorrowful legend of her daughter,
Persephone,
whose beauty so beguiled Hades,
the underworld god,
that he carried her away to his kingdom.
The grief-prostrated Demeter
heartbroken at the loss of her daughter
and the earth's crop was laid in waste.
Demeter's grief was soon allayed
when an arrangement was reached
where both Hades and Demeter
would share Persephone,
each to have her half the year.
What more poetic manner to be taught
the reason for the seasons?
When mother and daughter are together,
the earth flourishes,
and the earth's bounty once again
yields to man the fruits of his toils.

DEMETER AND THE FOODS FROM THE EARTH

GGGGGGGGGGGGGGGGGGGGGGGGGGGGGGGGGGGGGGGGGGGGGGGGGGGGGGGGGGGGGGGGGGGGGGGGGGGG

The terrain of Greece has challenged its farmers for thousands of years. It is a landscape of mountain ranges too steep to till, slender valleys too distant to reach, fertile coastlines too narrow to be worked by more than a few hands. As the population of ancient Greece grew, so did the need for wood to build its great trading ships and to fuel its foundries' fires; once the trees were cut, the rains washed much of the rich topsoil into the sea.

Farmers continue to cultivate the limited stretches of fertile soil and to await deliverance of the earth's, of Demeter's, bounty. They look forward to the harvest of the olive tree for its fruit and oil; of tomatoes and greens for salads; of legumes for cooking up in hearty soups; of shiny purple eggplant, green beans, and squash for stuffing or layering in elaborate vegetable dishes; of nuts and fruits for dozens of luscious sweets, and of wheat for breads, noodles, and delicate pastry sheets.

Soups

The ancient Greeks viewed a kettle of simmering soup as part of everyday life. From the writings of Athenaeus we learn that a lentil porridge was probably the most common soup of the times, unless one counts the Spartans' frugal "black broth" of pork, blood, and vinegar. Although this bitter brew was undoubtedly of little culinary merit, it did produce an old Greek saying my father often recalled: "When black broth was tasted by others, they said, 'No wonder the Spartans prefer to die, ten thousand times.' "

Today lentil and bean soups of all kinds remain popular, especially on village tables during the chilly autumn and winter months. Sunday dinner, whether in the city or the country, in Greece or in Greek immigrant homes around the world, always includes the celebrated *soupa avgolemono*, a zesty, golden mix of tangy lemon juice, freshly beaten eggs, rice, and rich chicken stock.

That same egg-lemon blend flavors dozens of other traditional soups, from celery heart to meatball to tripe. On Easter morning it is whisked into *mageritsa*, the variety-meat soup that traditionally breaks the long Lenten fast.

Chicken and Egg-Lemon Soup
Soupa Avgolemono

ᗺᗺᗺᗺᗺᗺᗺᗺᗺᗺᗺᗺᗺᗺᗺᗺᗺᗺᗺᗺᗺᗺᗺᗺᗺᗺᗺᗺᗺᗺ

*T*his is indisputably the queen of Greek soups. And at its heart is the most famous of all Greek sauces, the rich, lemony egg blend called *avgolemono*. You must work quickly and steadily, for constant beating is the secret to the success of this delicate soup.

2 quarts chicken stock
Salt, to taste
1 cup long-grain white rice
4 eggs
Juice of 2 lemons
Thin lemon slices, for garnish

In a large saucepan over high heat, bring stock and salt to a boil. Add rice, cover, reduce heat, and simmer 20 minutes.

Meanwhile, select 1 medium mixing bowl and 1 small one. Separate eggs, putting whites into larger bowl and yolks into smaller one. Beat whites until stiff peaks form. Whisk together yolks until blended, then slowly beat them into the whites. Gradually add lemon juice to eggs, beating continuously.

Remove stock mixture from heat. Slowly ladle 2 cups stock into beaten eggs, whisking continuously. Then pour egg mixture into saucepan. Place saucepan over low heat and stir to combine; do not boil.

Serve at once, garnished with lemon slices.

Serves 6 as a first course

Chilled Chicken and Egg-Lemon Soup
Soupa Krya Avgolemono

ᗺᗺᗺᗺᗺᗺᗺᗺᗺᗺᗺᗺᗺᗺᗺᗺᗺᗺᗺᗺᗺᗺᗺᗺᗺᗺᗺᗺᗺᗺ

*O*ffer guests a cup of this chilled cream soup before a main course of grilled fish and boiled young dandelion greens. Note that the dish needs to chill four to six hours.

2 cups chicken stock
2 teaspoons cornstarch
1 cup whipping cream
6 egg yolks
Juice of 3 lemons
Salt and white pepper
Freshly grated lemon zest or very thin
  lemon slices, for garnish

Place stock in a saucepan over medium-high heat and bring to a simmer; reduce heat to low. In a bowl add cornstarch to cream and stir to dissolve. Slowly add cream mixture to stock, stirring constantly over low heat until very smooth and creamy.

In a large bowl whisk egg yolks until pale yellow. Slowly add lemon juice to eggs, beating constantly; then gradually pour stock mixture into egg mixture, beating continuously. Cool to room temperature, cover, and chill 4 to 6 hours.

Adjust seasoning with salt and white pepper. Ladle soup into small bouillon cups and garnish with lemon zest.

Serves 4 to 6 as a first course

Celery and Egg-Lemon Soup
Soupa Selino Avgolemono

Only the tender heart of the celery plant is used in this lovely soup, but be sure to save some of the fragrant leaves for garnish.

4 cups chicken stock
2 medium celery hearts, chopped
Salt and freshly ground pepper, to taste
2 eggs
Juice of 1 lemon
Finely chopped celery leaves, for garnish

In a medium saucepan over high heat, bring stock and celery to a boil. Season with salt and pepper, cover, reduce heat, and simmer until celery is tender-crisp (about 5 minutes).

Meanwhile, select 1 medium mixing bowl and 1 small one. Separate eggs, putting whites into larger bowl and yolks into smaller one. Beat whites until stiff peaks form. Whisk yolks until blended, then slowly beat them into the whites. Gradually add lemon juice to eggs, beating continuously.

Remove stock mixture from heat. Slowly ladle 2 cups stock into beaten eggs, whisking continuously. Then pour egg mixture into saucepan. Place saucepan over low heat and stir to combine; do not boil.

Serve at once, garnished with celery leaves.

Serves 4 as a first course

Meatballs and Egg-Lemon Soup
Youvarlakia

*M*int-flecked meatballs in egg-lemon broth are a complete meal when served with crusty bread, feta slices, shiny black olives, and white wine.

1½ pounds lean ground lamb or beef
1 medium onion, grated
1 tablespoon minced fresh mint
½ cup long-grain white rice
4 eggs
Salt and freshly ground pepper, to taste
2 to 3 tablespoons finely minced fresh
*   parsley*
5 tablespoons butter
4 cups lamb or beef stock
Juice of 2 lemons

In a large bowl combine meat, onion, mint, rice, and 1 egg. Knead until ingredients are well blended. Season with salt and pepper. Form meat mixture into small balls about 1 inch in diameter. Spread parsley on a plate and roll balls in parsley to coat evenly on all sides.

In a dutch oven over medium heat, melt 3 tablespoons of the butter. Arrange meatballs in rows in bottom of pot and pour in stock, being careful not to disturb meatballs. Bring to a simmer, add the remaining butter, and season with salt and pepper. Cover and simmer over low heat until rice in meatballs is tender (35 to 40 minutes).

Meanwhile, select 1 medium mixing bowl and 1 small one. Separate the 3 remaining eggs, putting whites into larger bowl and yolks into smaller one. Beat whites until stiff peaks form. Whisk yolks until blended, then slowly beat them into the whites. Gradually add lemon juice to eggs, beating continuously.

Remove soup from heat. Slowly ladle 2 cups of the broth into beaten eggs, whisking continuously. Then pour egg mixture into soup. Place over low heat and stir to combine; do not boil. Serve immediately.

Serves 4 as an entrée

Tripe and Egg-Lemon Soup
Skembe Soupa

Throughout Greece there are small restaurants that specialize in tripe soup, which is eaten from early morning until late in the evening. The tripe requires long cooking, so plan your schedule accordingly.

1 pound honeycomb tripe
1 onion, quartered
2 bay leaves
1 clove garlic, halved
4 cups chicken stock
Salt and freshly ground pepper, to taste
2 eggs
Juice of 1 lemon

Rinse tripe well under cold water and drain. Place tripe in a medium saucepan and add onion, bay leaves, garlic, and water to cover. Bring to a boil and skim away any foam that forms on top. Reduce heat and simmer, uncovered, 2 hours, skimming occasionally. Drain, cut tripe in 1-inch-wide strips, and return to saucepan. Add chicken stock, bring to a boil, and simmer, uncovered, 30 minutes. Season with salt and pepper.

Select 1 medium mixing bowl and 1 small one. Separate eggs, putting whites into larger bowl and yolks into smaller one. Beat whites until stiff peaks form. Whisk yolks until blended, then slowly beat them into the whites. Gradually add lemon juice to eggs, beating continuously.

Remove soup from heat. Slowly ladle 2 cups of the soup broth into beaten eggs, whisking continuously. Then pour egg mixture into saucepan. Place saucepan over low heat and stir to combine; do not boil. Serve immediately.

Serves 4 as an entrée or 6 as a first course

Easter Soup

Mageritsa

The long Lenten fast is traditionally broken at the stroke of midnight with a bowl of this complex soup of variety meats bound with egg-lemon sauce. In Greece the lamb lungs and intestines are always included in the soup pot, but I have omitted them here because they are seldom found in North American markets.

1 pound honeycomb tripe
2 whole cloves
6 cups water
2 lamb hearts
1 pound each lambs' and calves' liver
Juice of 4 lemons
1 stalk celery, plus 1 cup finely chopped
   celery
1 yellow onion, quartered
Dash salt
Butter, for sautéing
2 bunches green onions (about 12;
   including some green top), finely
   chopped
½ cup finely chopped parsley
1 tablespoon dried dill, crushed
2 cups chicken stock
½ cup long-grain white rice
6 eggs

Rinse tripe well under cold water and drain. Place tripe, cloves, and 2 cups of the water in a medium saucepan. Bring to a boil and skim away any foam that forms on top. Reduce heat and simmer, uncovered, 30 minutes, skimming occasionally. Drain tripe, reserving cooking liquid; set tripe and cooking liquid aside.

Meanwhile, rinse hearts and livers under cold water and drain. Trim off any visible fat and connective tissue. Place hearts, livers, juice of 1 lemon, whole celery stalk, quartered onion, salt, and 2 cups of the water in a medium saucepan. Bring to a boil and skim away any foam that forms on top. Reduce heat and simmer, uncovered, 15 minutes, skimming off foam once or twice as needed. Drain, discarding vegetables and reserving meats and cooking liquid.

Finely chop reserved tripe, hearts, and livers. In a large, heavy-bottomed stock pot over medium heat, melt butter. Add chopped meats and sauté until browned (6 to 8 minutes). Add green onions, chopped celery, parsley, and dill; sauté a few minutes longer. Add reserved cooking liquids, chicken stock, and the remaining water. Bring to a boil, cover, reduce heat, and simmer 1 hour. Add rice, cover, and simmer 20 minutes.

Select 1 medium mixing bowl and 1 small one. Separate eggs, placing whites into larger bowl and yolks into smaller one. Beat whites until stiff peaks form. Whisk yolks until blended, then slowly beat them into the whites. Gradually add remaining lemon juice to eggs, beating continuously.

Remove soup from heat. Slowly ladle 2 cups of the broth into beaten eggs, whisking continuously. Then pour egg mixture into soup. Place stockpot over low heat and stir to combine; do not boil. Serve immediately.

Serves 8 to 10 as a first course

Bean Soup with Vegetables
Fassoulada

*T*he mention of *fassoulada* makes every Greek homesick. It brings back memories of joyful family gatherings, of everyone around the dinner table eating steaming bowls of this hearty soup. Accompany the soup with a platter of sliced onions, tomatoes, and feta dressed with olive oil, vinegar, and oregano. Note that the beans must be soaked overnight.

1 pound dried small white beans or
   black-eyed peas
½ cup olive oil
2 carrots, sliced lengthwise and then
   finely cubed
1 large onion, finely chopped
1 tablespoon chopped fresh parsley
1 cup finely chopped celery
2 cloves garlic, crushed
Dash dried mint, crushed
2 bay leaves
½ teaspoon dried fines herbes, crushed
1 cup Basic Tomato Sauce (see page 178)
Beef stock, as needed to cover
Salt and freshly ground pepper, to taste

Rinse beans and pick them over. Put beans in a large pot, add water to cover, and soak overnight.

In a large, heavy-bottomed stockpot over medium-high heat, warm oil. Add carrots, onion, parsley, celery, garlic, mint, bay leaves, and fines herbes; sauté until vegetables are golden brown (about 8 minutes). Drain beans and add to stockpot along with tomato sauce; stir well and add beef stock to cover by about 2 inches. Bring to a boil, cover, reduce heat, and simmer until beans are tender (about 1½ hours for white beans and 1 hour for black-eyed peas). Check periodically to make sure the beans are covered completely with liquid, adding water if necessary.

Adjust seasoning with salt and pepper and serve.

Serves 6 as an entrée

Lentil Soup
Soupa Faki

During the Lenten season this legume soup is popular fare. Serve with oven-fresh bread and boiled greens dressed with olive oil and lemon juice.

1 pound lentils
Olive oil, for sautéing
2 medium onions, chopped
3 stalks celery, chopped
2 small carrots, chopped
2 cloves garlic, minced
2 tablespoons tomato paste
2 bay leaves
1 tablespoon minced fresh oregano or
*　1 teaspoon dried oregano, crushed*
Salt and freshly ground pepper, to taste
½ cup red wine or red wine vinegar, or
*　to taste*

Rinse lentils and pick them over. In a large, heavy–bottomed stockpot over medium heat, warm oil. Add onions, celery, carrots, garlic, tomato paste, bay leaves, and oregano; sauté until onions are translucent (about 5 minutes). Add lentils and water to cover by about 3 inches. Bring to a boil, cover, reduce heat, and simmer until lentils are tender (about 30 minutes). Check periodically to make sure the lentils are covered completely with water, adding more if necessary.

Remove and discard bay leaves. Season with salt, pepper, and wine. Cover and let stand a few minutes to blend flavors, then serve.

Serves 6 as an entrée

Trahana Soup
Soupa Trahana

Homemade trahana, a pasta shaped like rice kernels, is a rarity. I compliment the Greek cooks of today who take the time to make this traditional pasta, which is usually dried for three or four days in the sun before it is added to soups or stews. Trahana is made with farina and flour and with milk and/or yogurt; yogurt gives it a taste reminiscent of sourdough bread. Ready-made trahana is found in Greek delicatessens and some specialty food shops.

1 can (16 oz) plum tomatoes with their
*　liquid*
1 onion, thinly sliced
2 stalks celery, finely chopped
1 bay leaf, crushed
2 cups chicken stock
1 cup trahana
1 cup dry white wine
Salt and freshly ground pepper, to taste

In a medium saucepan combine tomatoes and their liquid, onion, celery, bay leaf, and chicken stock. Bring to a boil and simmer a few minutes. Strain and return broth to saucepan.

Bring strained broth to a boil, add trahana, reduce heat, and simmer, uncovered, until very thick (about 20 minutes). Remove from heat and stir in wine. Cover and let stand a few minutes to blend flavors. Season with salt and pepper just before serving.

Serves 6 as a first course

Salads

A Greek dinner invariably includes a salad. It might be grilled eggplant seasoned with onion and garlic; tomatoes crisscrossed with anchovy fillets; lettuce leaves topped with jet black olives, tomato wedges, cucumbers, and capers; or young dandelion greens tossed with vinaigrette. The salad may precede or be eaten along with the main course.

In the early spring, when the choice of salad vegetables is limited, chunks of feta cheese are served atop seasonal greens and sprinkled with minced fresh herbs. Greeks will serve any herb, from oregano and mint, to thyme, dill, and rosemary, except one: basil.

Greeks hold basil in special esteem. A Greek home always has a pot of basil on a windowsill or balcony; the plant is tended with the care given a rare orchid. Songs eulogize the glories of the herb, and its heady fragrance permeates city streets and narrow village lanes.

Remember that for a Greek, a sprig of basil is a token of affection.

Athenian Salad

Salata Athenas

The proportions in this traditional Greek salad are not as critical as the arrangement of the ingredients, which should delight guests with its eye appeal. Like most Greeks, I chop the greens rather than tear them by hand. Kalamata olives, which are cured in brine and packed in vinegar, have a pleasantly sharp flavor; look for them in Greek groceries and well-stocked delicatessens.

Assorted greens (red and green leaf
*   lettuces, chicory, watercress)*
1 clove garlic, halved
Cucumbers, peeled and sliced
Green onions, thinly sliced
Capers
Radishes, thinly sliced
Tomatoes, peeled and quartered
Anchovy fillets
Kalamata olives and mint sprigs, for
*   garnish*
Feta Dressing Evoula (see page 180), as
*   needed*

Wash, dry, and coarsely chop greens. Rub a large wooden platter with cut sides of garlic. Arrange greens in center and cover them with rows of cucumber slices. Sprinkle onions and capers over the top, then surround with radish slices. Encircle edge of platter with tomato wedges, draping anchovy fillets at regular intervals in between the wedges. Garnish platter with olives and mint sprigs. Serve dressing in a bowl alongside.

Athenian Salad with Basic Vinaigrette Arrange salad ingredients as directed. Sprinkle salad with minced fresh oregano. Omit feta dressing; instead, drizzle with Basic Vinaigrette (see page 180), as needed.

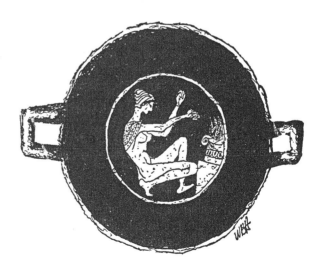

Eggplant Salad

Melitzanosalata

🆆🆆

*O*ffer this dish as a first course or as a side dish with grilled fish or roasted lamb. In the Greek countryside eggplants are sometimes cooked by tucking them next to hot fireplace coals, which gives them a wonderful smoky flavor. To achieve a similar result, cook the eggplants on a grill over a medium-hot charcoal fire.

2 medium (¾ to 1 lb each) eggplants
1 clove garlic, crushed
1 medium onion, grated
1 large tomato, peeled and chopped
1 tablespoon chopped fresh parsley
1 teaspoon each dried marjoram and
  dried fines herbes, crushed
Salt and freshly ground pepper, to taste
Olive oil, as needed
Romaine lettuce leaves, tomato wedges, and
  Kalamata olives, for accompaniment

Preheat oven to 350° F. Place eggplants on a baking sheet and bake until tender when pierced with a fork (about 45 minutes). Turn eggplants from time to time so they cook evenly. Remove from oven and let cool.

Peel eggplants; chop pulp and place in a bowl. Add garlic, onion, tomato, parsley, marjoram, fines herbes, salt, and pepper. Mix lightly, then add just enough oil to moisten and bind mixture. Mix well, cover, and chill.

Arrange lettuce leaves on a chilled platter and mound eggplant mixture in center. Surround with tomato wedges and olives.

Serves 4 as a side dish

Eggplant Dip To turn this salad into a dip, bake eggplants and combine with other ingredients as directed, omitting accompaniments. Transfer mixture to a food processor or blender. Purée, adding oil as needed to create dip consistency. Cover and chill; serve with bread or crackers.

Tomatoes with Feta Dressing

Domatosalata me Feta

🆆🆆🆆🆆🆆🆆🆆🆆🆆🆆🆆🆆🆆🆆🆆🆆🆆🆆🆆🆆🆆🆆🆆🆆🆆🆆🆆🆆🆆🆆🆆🆆🆆🆆🆆🆆🆆🆆

*I*n this hot-weather salad, a tangy dressing made with feta bathes ripe red tomatoes. Allow time for chilling the ingredients. The dressing can be made in advance and stored in the refrigerator up to 10 days.

Red or green lettuce leaves, chilled, to
  line platter
4 large, ripe tomatoes, chilled
Kalamata olives, for garnish
Feta Dressing Evoula (see page 180)

Line a platter with lettuce leaves. Slice tomatoes and arrange in even rows over lettuce. Garnish with olives and serve dressing in a bowl on the side.

Serves 4 as a side dish

Tomatoes with Anchovies and Capers

Domatosalata me Sardeles

🔲🔲🔲🔲🔲🔲🔲🔲🔲🔲🔲🔲🔲🔲🔲🔲🔲🔲🔲🔲🔲🔲🔲🔲🔲🔲🔲🔲🔲🔲

*H*ere, pleasantly salty anchovy fillets act as the perfect counterpoint to the natural sweetness of vine-ripened tomatoes. Wash, dry, and chill the lettuce leaves a couple of hours before serving the salad so that they will be very crisp.

> *Romaine lettuce leaves, chilled, to line*
> *   platter*
> *4 ripe tomatoes, chilled*
> *¼ cup olive oil*
> *2 tablespoons wine vinegar*
> *1 tablespoon minced fresh oregano*
> *Salt and freshly ground pepper, to taste*
> *2 tins (2 oz each) anchovy fillets rolled*
> *   with capers, drained*

Line a platter with lettuce leaves. Slice tomatoes and arrange over leaves.

In a small bowl whisk together oil, vinegar, oregano, salt, and pepper; pour dressing over tomato slices. Scatter rolled anchovy fillets over the top and serve at once.

Serves 4 as a side dish

Cucumbers with Yogurt

Angourosalata me Yiaourti

🔲🔲🔲🔲🔲🔲🔲🔲🔲🔲🔲🔲🔲🔲🔲🔲🔲🔲🔲🔲🔲🔲🔲🔲🔲🔲🔲🔲🔲🔲

*I*f you haven't any homemade yogurt on hand, high-quality commercial yogurt may be substituted. This salad is an ideal accompaniment to grilled fish. Allow time for it to chill thoroughly before serving.

> *4 medium cucumbers*
> *1 clove garlic, minced*
> *1 medium onion, grated*
> *3 cups Homemade Yogurt (see page 181)*
> *Salt and freshly ground pepper, to taste*
> *1 tablespoon minced fresh parsley*

Peel 3 of the cucumbers and force through large holes of a vegetable grater into a large mixing bowl. Add garlic, onion, and yogurt; mix well. Season with salt and pepper.

Do not peel remaining cucumber. With fork tines score skin lengthwise; thinly slice cucumber crosswise. Mound yogurt-cucumber mixture in a serving bowl and garnish with cucumber slices. Sprinkle with parsley, cover, and chill before serving.

Serves 4 to 6 as a side dish

Seafood Salad with Mayonnaise
Psari Salata me Mayoneza

*F*resh lobster and shrimp signal a special occasion. Allow time for the cooked seafood to chill before assembling the salad. To make individual salads, line each plate with a lettuce leaf, cover with a bed of shredded lettuce, and mound shellfish mixture on top.

Homemade Mayonnaise (see page 181)
1 large (about 2 lb) live lobster
1 pound medium shrimp in their shells
Green leaf lettuce, chilled, as needed
½ cup chopped green onion
½ cup chopped celery
2 tablespoons olive oil
3 lemons
Salt and freshly ground pepper, to taste
1 tablespoon minced fresh oregano
2 hard-cooked eggs, sliced, and capers,
  for garnish

Prepare mayonnaise; cover and chill.

Bring a large pot filled with water to a boil. Drop in lobster; cook until shell turns bright red and a leg pulls off easily (10 to 15 minutes). Drain and cool under running water; remove shell and cut meat in cubes. It should equal about 2 cups; cover and chill.

Bring a saucepan filled with water to a boil. Drop in shrimp and cook until their shells change color and become opaque. Drain and cool under running water; peel and devein. Cover and chill.

In a shallow salad platter, arrange a bed of lettuce leaves. In a mixing bowl combine lobster, shrimp, onion, celery, oil, juice of 1 lemon, salt, and pepper; stir gently to combine. Mound seafood mixture on lettuce leaves and sprinkle with oregano. Cut remaining 2 lemons in wedges and place around salad. Garnish with eggs and capers. Serve mayonnaise in a bowl alongside.

Serves 4 as a light entrée

Beet and Onion Salad

Kokinogoulia Salata

GGGGGGGGGGGGGGGGGGGGGGGGGGGGGGGGGGGG

Small beets are generally sweeter and have a better texture than large ones. Save the green beet tops, boil them until tender, and dress with olive oil and lemon juice for a vegetable side dish. Allow time for the salad to chill before serving.

2 bunches (about 1 lb each) small beets
2 onions, sliced in thin rings
2 cloves garlic, minced
2 bay leaves
Salt and freshly ground pepper, to taste
½ cup olive oil
½ cup red wine vinegar

Trim stems from beets, leaving about ¼ inch of stem attached. Place beets in a large saucepan and add water to cover. Bring to boil, cover, reduce heat, and simmer until tender when pierced with a fork (about 25 minutes, depending upon size). Drain and cool. Peel and slice in rounds about ¼ inch thick.

Arrange beets on a platter and top with onion rings. Sprinkle garlic over the top. Break bay leaves in half and tuck in among the beets. Sprinkle liberally with salt and pepper. In a small bowl whisk together oil and vinegar and pour over salad. Chill well before serving.

Serves 6 as a side dish

Avocado with Fish Roe Purée

Avocado me Taramosalata

GGGGGGGGGGGGGGGGGGGGGGGGGGGGGGGGGGGGGGG

The classic fish roe purée called *taramosalata* here serves as the centerpiece of an elegant first-course salad that is dressed by each diner with a squeeze of fresh lemon juice. Do not cut the avocados until just before serving time or they will darken.

8 large lettuce leaves, chilled
2 ripe avocados
6 tablespoons Fish Roe Purée (see page 22)
2 lemons
8 Kalamata olives
1 teaspoon minced fresh parsley

Arrange 2 lettuce leaves on each of 4 individual salad plates. Cut avocados in half lengthwise, remove and discard pits, and peel. Place one avocado half, cut side up, in the center of each serving plate. Spoon 1½ tablespoons of the roe mixture into the hollow of each avocado half.

Cut each lemon in 4 wedges; set 2 wedges on each plate, along with 2 olives. Sprinkle parsley over salad and serve.

Serves 4 as a first course

Hot Potato Salad
Zesti Patatosalata

GGGGGGGGGGGGGGGGGGGGGGGGGGGGGGGGGGGGGG

*L*et the potatoes cool as little as possible before peeling; this salad tastes best hot. Also, the potatoes absorb the flavors of the dressing better when still very warm.

4 large potatoes
½ cup olive oil
¼ cup wine vinegar
Salt and freshly ground pepper, to taste
6 green onions (including some green
    top), finely chopped
1 tablespoon minced fresh oregano
Finely minced fresh parsley, for garnish

Place potatoes in a large saucepan, add water to cover, and bring to a boil. Cook until tender when pierced with a fork (about 40 minutes). Drain.

When potatoes are just cool enough to handle, peel and cut lengthwise in quarters. Arrange warm quarters on a heated platter. In a small bowl whisk together oil, vinegar, salt, and pepper; pour over potatoes. Sprinkle with onions and oregano and garnish with parsley. Serve immediately.

Serves 6 as a side dish

Cabbage Salad
Lahano salata

GGGGGGGGGGGGGGGGGGGGGGGGGGGGGGGGGGGGGGGG

*B*oth the common green head cabbage and the paler green, crinkly leaved savoy variety will work beautifully for this salad. The savoy is milder in flavor, so you may want to reduce the amount of vinegar in the dressing. Allow time for the salad to chill before serving.

1 medium (about 1½ lb) green cabbage,
    finely shredded
1 medium onion, grated
2 tablespoons chopped fresh parsley
⅓ cup olive oil, or to taste
3 tablespoons wine vinegar, or to taste
1 teaspoon sugar
Salt and freshly ground pepper, to taste
1 green bell pepper, seeded, deribbed,
    and cut in thin rings, for garnish

In a large salad bowl, combine cabbage, onion, and parsley. In a small bowl whisk together oil, vinegar, sugar, salt, and ground pepper. Pour dressing over cabbage and toss until thoroughly coated. Arrange bell pepper rings on top. Cover and chill before serving.

Serves 4 to 6 as a side dish

Vegetable Entrées and Side Dishes

Taste a vegetable fresh from the garden and you will be forever haunted by the purity of its flavor. In Greece, as elsewhere, homegrown vegetables spoil your palate for anything cultivated commercially. So every Greek with a patch of soil tends whatever he or she can—ruffly escarole, deep-green spinach, tender zucchini, ruby red tomatoes, thorny-topped artichokes, dusty-green okra pods.

The harvest will appear in a myriad of guises: boiled greens bathed in fruity olive oil and tart lemon juice, golden vegetable fritters with a thick garlicky sauce, a rich eggplant and lamb casserole, rice-stuffed cabbage leaves, or an artichoke omelet. The recipes that follow range from hearty vegetable and meat entrées to simple side dishes.

Baked Eggplant with Lamb
Moussaka

• ∞ •

*E*ggplant stars in dishes throughout the Mediterranean, but none surpasses the fame of Greek moussaka. Some food historians believe that this elaborately layered meat-and-vegetable casserole was adapted from *maghmuma*, a similar mixture of lamb, onion, and eggplant that was common fare on the tables of the tenth-century caliphs of Baghdad. The semihard, tangy *kefalotyri* cheese can be found in Greek delicatessens.

> *3 medium eggplants*
> *Salt*
> *¼ cup butter*
> *2 pounds ground lamb*
> *Freshly ground pepper, to taste*
> *2 onions, chopped*
> *3 cloves garlic, minced*
> *¼ teaspoon each ground cinnamon and*
> *   freshly grated nutmeg*
> *½ teaspoon dried fines herbes, crushed*
> *2 tablespoons minced fresh parsley*
> *1 cup Basic Tomato Sauce (see page 178)*
> *½ cup red wine*
> *4 cups Basic White Sauce (see page 174)*
> *3 egg yolks (optional)*
> *Olive oil, for frying and for baking dish*
> *About 1½ cups freshly grated kefalotyri*
> *   or Parmesan cheese*

Peel eggplants and cut lengthwise in ½-inch-thick slices. Liberally sprinkle with salt, place on paper towels, weight down with a heavy platter, and let stand to drain 30 minutes to 1 hour.

In a large skillet over medium-high heat, melt butter. Add lamb, pepper, onions, garlic, and salt to taste; sauté until meat is evenly browned (about 10 minutes), breaking it up with a fork as it cooks. Add cinnamon, nutmeg, fines herbes, parsley, and tomato sauce; stir, mixing well. Add wine and simmer, uncovered, until liquid is reduced and mixture is quite thick (about 20 minutes). Remove from heat and set aside.

While lamb mixture simmers, prepare white sauce. For a richer sauce, beat the optional egg yolks in a small bowl and whisk in some of the hot sauce. Add egg mixture to remaining white sauce and whisk to blend well. Set aside.

Preheat oven to 350° F. Wipe eggplant slices dry. With a pastry brush, lightly oil a skillet placed over high heat. Quickly fry eggplant slices until golden on both sides but still firm; remove to paper towels to drain. (If you follow this method closely the eggplant will not absorb too much oil.)

Lightly oil a 9- by 13-inch baking dish. Layer half of the eggplant in bottom of dish. Spoon lamb mixture over eggplant, sprinkle with a layer of cheese, and then top with remaining eggplant. Sprinkle with more cheese and then pour reserved white sauce evenly over the casserole. Lavishly sprinkle cheese over the top. Bake until cheese is golden brown (20 to 30 minutes). Do not overcook or eggplant will be too soft.

Cool slightly, then cut in 3-inch squares to serve. (See variations on page 49.)

Serves 12 as an entrée

Zucchini Variation For the eggplant, substitute 2 pounds zucchini, sliced lengthwise and fried briefly in olive oil.

Potato Variation For the eggplant, substitute 2 pounds potatoes, cut in ¼-inch-thick slices and fried a few minutes in olive oil.

Spinach-Cheese Pie
Spanakopeta

*R*ead the tips on working with filo dough (see page 14) before starting this recipe. *Spanakopeta* may be served hot or at room temperature. Offer it as an appetizer in small squares, a vegetable side dish in larger squares, or even as a separate course following the entrée. A single-edged razor blade is the best tool for slicing this crispy pie in serving pieces. This recipe makes approximately six cups of spinach filling, which can also be used to stuff filo triangles (see page 17 to 19).

> 3 pounds spinach
> ¾ cup olive oil
> 2 bunches (about 12) green onions,
>   finely chopped
> ½ cup minced fresh parsley
> 2 teaspoons minced fresh dill or ½
>   teaspoon dried dill, crushed (optional)
> 8 eggs, beaten
> 1 pound feta cheese, crumbled
> Salt, to taste
> 1 cup butter, melted and cooled
> ½ pound filo dough, thawed overnight in
>   refrigerator if frozen

Rinse spinach well, trim off stems, and dry leaves thoroughly with paper towels; chop finely and set aside.

Preheat oven to 350° F. In a small skillet over medium-high heat, warm ¼ cup of the oil. Add onions and sauté until golden (about 6 minutes). In a large mixing bowl combine spinach, parsley, dill, eggs, and cheese. Add hot cooked green onions, season lightly with salt, and mix well.

Brush a 9- by 13-inch baking dish with some of the melted butter. Unfold filo dough so it lays flat, then cover to prevent it from drying out. Combine butter and the remaining oil. Line baking dish with 5 filo sheets, brushing each with some of the butter-oil mixture. Spread spinach mixture over filo and top with remaining filo sheets, brushing each with some of the butter-oil mixture. Lavishly brush top sheet with butter-oil mixture.

Bake until golden brown (about 45 minutes). Cool slightly, then cut in squares to serve.

Serves 12 as a side dish or 8 as an entrée

Stuffed Zucchini
Papoutsakia

The Greeks stuff a wide variety of vegetables, but zucchini are among the easiest to prepare. For an even simpler version of *papoutsakia* ("little shoes"), substitute slices of feta cheese for the white sauce.

4 medium zucchini of uniform size
Salt, to taste
Butter, for sautéing
1 small onion, finely chopped
1 clove garlic, minced
¼ pound lean ground beef
2 tablespoons minced fresh parsley
½ tablespoon minced fresh oregano
Freshly ground pepper, to taste
2 tablespoons dry white wine
Hot water, as needed
1 cup Basic White Sauce (see page 174)
Freshly grated kefalotyri or Parmesan
  cheese

Trim ends off zucchini but leave whole. Bring a large saucepan of salted water to a boil. Add zucchini and boil until half-cooked (about 7 minutes). Drain, cut zucchini in half lengthwise, and carefully scoop out pulp, forming a ¼-inch-thick shell. Chop pulp finely; set shells and pulp aside.

Preheat oven to 350° F. In a skillet over medium heat, melt butter. Add onion, garlic, and beef and sauté until beef is lightly browned (about 7 minutes). Add ½ cup of the zucchini pulp (reserve remaining pulp for another use), parsley, oregano, salt, pepper, and wine. Simmer, uncovered, until liquid evaporates (about 20 minutes).

Sprinkle zucchini shells lightly with salt and pepper and fill them with beef mixture. Arrange stuffed zucchini close together in a baking pan. Pour hot water to a depth of ½ inch in bottom of pan. Spoon 2 tablespoons white sauce atop each stuffed zucchini. Sprinkle tops lightly with cheese.

Bake until sauce is browned and zucchini is tender when pierced with a fork (about 25 minutes). Serve hot.

Serves 4 as an entrée or 8 as a side dish

Eggplant Variation Substitute 4 Japanese eggplants for zucchini. Trim ends; cut in half lengthwise and scoop out pulp. Sauté shells gently in butter to soften. Proceed as directed for zucchini, using ½ cup chopped eggplant pulp in filling.

Tomatoes Stuffed with Beef and Zucchini
Domates Yemistes

Large, firm, vine-ripened tomatoes of uniform size are best for stuffing. For an entrée, serve each person two of these beef-filled tomatoes; accompany with sliced cucumbers, assorted Greek cheeses, olives, and a bottle of chilled white retsina.

12 large, ripe tomatoes
8 tablespoons olive oil
3 medium onions, finely minced
1 clove garlic, minced
1 pound lean ground beef
1 cup finely shredded, unpeeled
  zucchini
½ cup minced fresh parsley
1 cup long-grain white rice
½ cup pine nuts
1 cup dry white wine
Salt and freshly ground pepper, to taste
1 tablespoon minced fresh oregano or 1
  teaspoon dried oregano, crushed
1 cup water

Cut ½ inch off tops of tomatoes; reserve tops and scoop out pulp from bottoms, forming shells about ⅓ inch thick. Turn bottoms upside down on a wire rack to drain; chop pulp finely and set aside.

Preheat oven to 350° F. In a skillet over medium-high heat, warm 2 tablespoons of the oil. Add onions, garlic, and beef; sauté until beef is lightly browned (about 6 minutes), breaking meat up with a fork as it cooks. Add zucchini, parsley, rice, pine nuts, 1 cup of the tomato pulp, ½ cup of the wine, salt, and pepper; simmer, uncovered, 30 minutes. Remove from heat and cool slightly.

Turn tomato shells upright and sprinkle interiors lightly with salt, pepper, and oregano. Spoon beef mixture into tomatoes and cover with reserved tops. Place close together in a baking pan. Combine the water and the remaining tomato pulp, oil, and white wine. Spoon mixture over tomatoes and bake until tomatoes are very tender when pierced with a fork (about 35 minutes), basting occasionally with pan juices.

To serve, transfer tomatoes to a large serving platter or individual plates and spoon pan juices over the top.

Serves 6 as an entrée or 12 as a side dish

Tomatoes Stuffed with Rice

Domates Yemistes me Rizi

These dill-scented stuffed tomatoes complement grilled fish or roasted meats. They are delicious straight from the oven or at room temperature.

10 medium tomatoes
1 cup olive oil
2 onions, finely chopped
2 tablespoons chopped fresh parsley
1 clove garlic, minced
2 tablespoons minced fresh dill
1½ tablespoons minced fresh oregano
1 cup long-grain white rice
½ cup pine nuts
Salt and freshly ground pepper, to taste
2 tablespoons tomato paste
¾ cup dry white wine
Sugar, for sprinkling
½ cup hot water

Cut off ½ inch from tops of tomatoes. Reserve tops and scoop out pulp from bottoms, forming shells about ⅓ inch thick. Turn shells upside down on a wire rack to drain; chop pulp finely and set aside.

Preheat oven to 350° F. In a skillet over medium-high heat, warm ¼ cup of the oil. Add onions and sauté until golden (about 7 minutes). Add reserved tomato pulp, parsley, garlic, dill, 1 tablespoon of the oregano, rice, pine nuts, salt, and pepper. Stir well. Dilute tomato paste in ½ cup of the wine and add to skillet. Cover and simmer 20 minutes.

Turn tomato shells upright and sprinkle interiors with salt, pepper, and sugar. Stuff tomatoes with rice mixture and cover with reserved tops. Place close together in a baking pan. Drizzle the remaining oil over tomatoes, sprinkle with the remaining oregano, and splash with the remaining wine. Pour the water into the pan.

Bake until tomatoes are very tender when pierced with a fork (about 35 minutes), basting frequently with pan juices.

Serves 5 as an entrée or 8 to 10 as a side dish

Stuffed Cabbage
Lahanodolmades

Cooks around the world claim their country's cabbage rolls to be the finest. We Greeks are equally partisan about these plump packets of mixed meat seasoned with mint and cinnamon.

1 large (about 2½ lb) green cabbage
½ pound each lean ground lamb and beef
1 egg
1 onion, finely chopped
1 clove garlic, minced
2 teaspoons minced fresh oregano
1 tablespoon minced fresh mint
¼ teaspoon ground cinnamon
¾ cup long-grain white rice
2 tablespoons tomato paste
3 tablespoons plus ½ cup olive oil
½ cup dry white wine
Salt and freshly ground pepper, to taste
1 cup Basic Tomato Sauce (see page 178)
1 bay leaf, crushed
2 cups beef stock

To prepare cabbage cut out tough portion of core but leave head intact. Bring a large pot of water to a boil and immerse cabbage in it. Parboil 5 minutes, then turn off heat and let cabbage stand in water 5 minutes. Drain, and when cool enough to handle, separate into leaves. Chop small interior leaves and the tender core; set chopped cabbage and whole leaves aside.

In a large mixing bowl combine lamb, beef, egg, onion, garlic, oregano, mint, cinnamon, rice, tomato paste, the 3 tablespoons olive oil, wine, salt, and pepper. Knead with hands until well mixed.

Line the bottom of a dutch oven with the chopped cabbage. Stack whole leaves on a flat surface. Spoon about 1 tablespoon (amount depends on size of leaf) of the meat mixture in center of each leaf. Fold over base to cover filling, fold in sides, then loosely roll up into a compact bundle. Secure with a toothpick if packet doesn't want to stay closed. Arrange a layer of stuffed leaves, seam side down, on the bed of cabbage. Sprinkle with some of the ½ cup olive oil, tomato sauce, bay leaf, salt, and pepper. Repeat layering until all of the cabbage rolls are in the pot, sprinkling each layer in same manner as the first.

Combine beef stock and any remaining tomato sauce and oil and pour over rolls; add water as needed just to cover rolls.

Bring to a boil and cover pot. Reduce heat to low and simmer until filling is cooked and cabbage leaves are very tender (about 1 hour). Serve rolls with cooking liquid spooned over them.

Serves 6 to 8 as an entrée

Egg-Lemon Sauce Variation Assemble and cook rolls, omitting tomato sauce. Double the recipe for Egg-Lemon Sauce (see page 173), using stock in which rolls were cooked as part of the liquid. Serve cabbage rolls with Egg-Lemon Sauce spooned over them.

Apples Stuffed with Raisins and Nuts

Mila Yemistes

🅖🅖🅖🅖🅖🅖🅖🅖🅖🅖🅖🅖🅖🅖🅖🅖🅖🅖🅖🅖🅖🅖🅖🅖🅖🅖🅖🅖🅖🅖

Although this recipe is based on a fruit rather than a vegetable, it appears here with the stuffed vegetables because it is a traditional savory side dish. Any large, firm-fleshed apple variety, such as Rome Beauty or Winesap, can be used. Chill stuffed apples well before serving. These apples make a delicious accompaniment to game or pork entrées.

6 large apples
2 tablespoons raisins
4 dried figs, minced
2 tablespoons each chopped walnuts and
*   slivered blanched almonds*
¼ teaspoon ground cinnamon
¼ cup sugar
¼ cup brandy
Freshly grated nutmeg, to taste
1 cup water

Preheat oven to 350° F. Cut off and discard ¾-inch slice from top of each apple. Core apples, then scoop out pulp, forming ⅓-inch-thick shells. Finely chop pulp and place in a mixing bowl. Add remaining ingredients except nutmeg and the water; mix well.

Stuff apple shells with pulp mixture. Place apples close together in a baking pan. Dust tops lightly with nutmeg. Pour the water into the pan, then cover pan tightly with aluminum foil. Bake until apples are tender when pierced with a fork (about 20 minutes). Cool and chill before serving.

Serves 6

Artichoke Omelet

Avga me Anginares

🅖🅖🅖🅖🅖🅖🅖🅖🅖🅖🅖🅖🅖🅖🅖🅖🅖🅖🅖🅖🅖🅖🅖🅖🅖🅖🅖🅖🅖🅖

Because the beauty of omelets is that they are quick to prepare, I recommend using frozen artichoke hearts here rather than fresh ones. The artichokes are mixed with the eggs and the omelet is served unfolded, in classic Greek style. Serve with a side dish of tomato slices sprinkled with crumbled feta and drizzled with olive oil.

Butter, for sautéing
1 package (10 oz) frozen artichoke
*   hearts, thawed and well drained*
4 green onions (including some green
*   top), chopped*
1 tablespoon minced fresh parsley
Salt and freshly ground pepper, to taste
2 tablespoons olive oil
8 eggs, beaten

In a large skillet over medium heat, melt enough butter to form a thin coating on bottom of pan. Add artichoke hearts and sauté lightly on all sides. Do not stir artichokes; instead gently shake the pan to keep them from sticking, adding more butter if necessary. Add green onions, parsley, salt, and pepper; cover and cook over low heat until artichokes are tender when pierced with a fork.

Raise heat and drizzle oil over artichokes. When oil is hot pour in eggs, distributing them with a spatula so they evenly cover the artichokes. Reduce heat to low, cover, and cook until eggs are set but still moist, or until done to your liking. Gently slide onto a heated platter to serve.

Serves 4 as a light entrée

Tomatoes and Eggs
Avga me Domates

🝙🝙🝙🝙🝙🝙🝙🝙🝙🝙🝙🝙🝙🝙🝙🝙🝙🝙🝙🝙🝙🝙🝙🝙🝙🝙🝙🝙🝙🝙🝙🝙🝙

*H*ere is a modest dish that retains the natural flavors of its fresh ingredients. To achieve a creamy consistency, gently fold the eggs into the tomatoes in a circular motion.

> *3 tablespoons olive oil*
> *3 medium-sized ripe tomatoes, peeled,*
> *   seeded, and chopped*
> *Salt and freshly ground pepper*
> *1 teaspoon minced fresh oregano*
> *2 tablespoons butter*
> *1 teaspoon cornstarch*
> *1 tablespoon water*
> *8 eggs, beaten*

In a skillet over medium heat, warm oil. Add tomatoes and sauté gently 5 minutes. Season with salt, pepper, and oregano; cook 3 or 4 minutes longer. Stir in butter.

While tomatoes are cooking, dissolve cornstarch in water and whisk into eggs; season with salt and pepper. Raise heat to medium-high and pour eggs into skillet to cover tomatoes evenly. Allow eggs to cook slightly, reduce heat, and gently fold eggs into tomatoes in a circular motion. Cook until set but still moist, or until done to your liking. Serve on a heated platter.

Serves 3 or 4 as a light entrée

Zucchini and Eggs
Avga me Kolokithaki

🝙🝙🝙🝙🝙🝙🝙🝙🝙🝙🝙🝙🝙🝙🝙🝙🝙🝙🝙🝙🝙🝙🝙🝙🝙🝙🝙🝙🝙🝙🝙🝙🝙🝙🝙🝙

*A*lmost every Greek village household has its own small vegetable garden—rows of ripening egg plants, tomatoes, green beans, and, in the earliest days of summer, young, pale green zucchini.

> *Butter, for sautéing*
> *4 medium zucchini, thinly sliced*
> *1 onion, grated*
> *Salt and freshly ground pepper, to taste*
> *1 teaspoon minced fresh oregano*
> *8 eggs, beaten*

In a skillet over medium heat, melt enough butter to form a thin coating on bottom of pan. Add zucchini and onion and sauté until onion is translucent (about 5 minutes). Sprinkle with salt, pepper, and oregano; continue sautéing until zucchini is golden (about 5 minutes), turning slices over to cook them evenly.

Add a bit more butter to pan if it seems dry and pour in eggs to cover zucchini evenly. Cook until eggs are set but still moist, lifting edges of zucchini slices to allow uncooked egg to flow underneath. Gently slide onto a heated platter to serve.

Serves 4 as a light entrée

Spinach and Rice
Spanakorizo

🏛🏛🏛🏛🏛🏛🏛🏛🏛🏛🏛🏛🏛🏛🏛🏛🏛🏛🏛🏛🏛🏛🏛🏛🏛🏛🏛🏛🏛🏛🏛

*U*sually this dish comes to the table hot from the pan, but I find it to be just as satisfying when it is served at room temperature.

> *2 pounds spinach*
> *⅓ cup olive oil*
> *2 medium onions, minced*
> *1 small clove garlic, minced*
> *1 cup long-grain white rice*
> *2 tablespoons tomato paste*
> *2 bay leaves*
> *Salt and freshly ground pepper, to taste*
> *2 cups beef stock*

Rinse spinach well and trim off stems; dry leaves thoroughly with paper towels. Tear in small pieces and set aside.

In a heavy-bottomed saucepan over medium-high heat, warm oil. Add onions, garlic, and rice; sauté until onions are translucent (about 5 minutes). Stir in tomato paste, then add reserved spinach, bay leaves, salt, and pepper. Mix well and pour in stock.

Cover and simmer over low heat until rice is tender and liquid is absorbed (about 20 minutes). Discard bay leaves before serving.

Serves 6 as a side dish

Mixed Vegetable Casserole

🏛🏛🏛🏛🏛🏛🏛🏛🏛🏛🏛🏛🏛🏛🏛🏛🏛🏛🏛🏛🏛🏛🏛🏛🏛🏛🏛🏛🏛🏛🏛

*T*his dish calls on you to use your culinary imagination to combine the best of the seasonal produce available.

> *1 can (28 oz) plum tomatoes*
> *2 cloves garlic, minced*
> *3 tablespoons plus ¾ cup olive oil*
> *1 pound potatoes, peeled and sliced*
> *⅛ inch thick*
> *2 large carrots, peeled and sliced ⅛ inch*
> *thick*
> *1½ pounds zucchini, sliced ¼ inch thick*
> *2 onions, sliced*
> *2 pounds okra, stems trimmed*
> *Salt and freshly ground pepper, to taste*
> *1½ tablespoons minced fresh oregano*
> *½ cup chopped fresh parsley*

Drain tomatoes, catching their liquid in a medium bowl. Chop tomatoes and return to their liquid. Add garlic; set mixture aside.

Preheat oven to 350° F. Pour the 3 tablespoons oil into a large dutch oven, tipping pot to cover bottom evenly. Layer half of the potatoes, then carrots, zucchini, onions, and okra, drizzling each layer with some of the ¾ cup oil and some of the tomato mixture. Sprinkle the layer with salt and pepper and some of the oregano and parsley. Repeat layers, drizzling each layer with oil and tomato mixture and sprinkling with salt and pepper. Pour the remaining oil and tomato mixture evenly over the top.

Cover pan tightly and bake until vegetables are tender (about 1 hour).

Serves 6 as a side dish

Artichokes and Rice

Anginares Pilafi

The Mediterranean region is home to the artichoke and the Greeks treat this native with great respect. Here tender young artichokes are cooked in chicken stock with rice and fresh herbs. Serve this dish as an accompaniment to roasted chicken or lamb.

Juice of 2 lemons
6 small artichokes
8 tablespoons olive oil
1 onion, minced
3 tablespoons chopped fresh parsley
2 tablespoons finely chopped fresh dill
2 cups chicken stock
1 cup long-grain white rice

Fill a large bowl with water and add juice of 1 lemon. Rinse artichokes under cold water and remove 3 or 4 outer layers of leaves. Slice 1 inch off leaf tops; trim stems. Cut artichokes in quarters lengthwise, remove thistles with a spoon, and drop quarters into the bowl of acidulated water.

In a heavy-bottomed saucepan over medium-high heat, warm 5 tablespoons of the oil. Add onion, parsley, and dill; sauté until onion is translucent (about 5 minutes). Drain artichokes and add them to saucepan with onion mixture; sauté 5 minutes. Add stock and bring to a boil. Cover, reduce heat, and simmer until artichokes are half-cooked (about 15 minutes).

Add rice, stir gently, cover, and simmer until rice is cooked and liquid is absorbed (about 20 minutes).

Transfer to a serving dish and sprinkle with juice of the remaining lemon. In a small skillet heat the remaining oil to smoking point and drizzle over the top. Cover and let stand 5 minutes, then serve.

Serves 6 as a side dish

Lima Bean Plaki

Lopia Plaki

Plaki refers to a traditional method of cooking vegetables or seafood in a highly seasoned sauce based on onions, parsley, olive oil, and tomatoes. Dishes prepared in this style may be cooked in the oven or on the stove-top. Serve this version hot or at room temperature as an accompaniment to roasted meats or grilled fish. Begin soaking the beans the night before you plan to cook them.

1 pound dried lima beans
¾ cup olive oil
1 onion, finely chopped
2 cloves garlic, minced
2 carrots, finely chopped
1 stalk celery, finely chopped
½ cup chopped fresh parsley
2 tablespoons chopped fresh dill or
   2 teaspoons dried dill, crushed
1 teaspoon dried fines herbes, crushed
Juice of 1 lemon
1 can (16 oz) plum tomatoes, with their
   liquid
2 cups chicken stock
Salt and freshly ground pepper, to taste
2 cups water

Rinse and pick over beans. Soak in water to cover overnight; drain.

Place beans in a saucepan with water to cover, bring to a boil, and parboil 25 minutes. Drain and set aside.

In a dutch oven over medium-high heat, warm oil. Add onion, garlic, carrots, celery, and parsley; sauté until onion is translucent (about 5 minutes). Add dill, fines herbes, lemon juice, tomatoes, stock, salt, and pepper. Bring to a boil, reduce heat, and simmer 20 minutes. Add drained beans and the water; simmer until beans are tender (about 25 minutes).

Serves 6 to 8 as a side dish

Okra Braised with Tomatoes

Bamyes Yahni

Although okra is native to Africa, the Greeks have embraced it warmly, adding it to chicken and lamb stews or braising it with fresh tomatoes, as in this recipe. Trim the stems from the okra but do not pierce the pods. If you do, the pods will "bleed" and make the sauce mucilaginous.

    3 tablespoons olive oil
    1 small onion, minced
    1 clove garlic, minced
    1 tablespoon chopped fresh parsley
    2 ripe tomatoes, peeled, seeded, and
        diced
    2 tablespoons dry white wine
    1 cup chicken stock
    2 pounds okra, stems trimmed
    Salt and freshly ground pepper, to taste

In a large skillet over medium-high heat, warm oil. Add onion, garlic, and parsley and sauté until onion is translucent (about 5 minutes). Stir in tomatoes, wine, and stock; cook a few minutes longer to blend flavors.

Add okra to pan, spoon the pan juices over the top, and season with salt and pepper. Cover and simmer over medium-low heat until okra is very tender (about 20 minutes).

Serves 6 as a side dish

Carrots Sautéed in Butter

Karota Tighanita

Sweet young carrots need little additional flavoring, just a buttery glaze and a smattering of fresh herbs.

    12 to 15 young carrots (each about
        5 in. long)
    6 tablespoons butter
    4 green onions, finely chopped
    3 tablespoons minced fresh parsley, plus
        minced fresh parsley for garnish
    Dash each minced fresh thyme and
        oregano
    ½ teaspoon sugar
    2 tablespoons dry white wine
    Salt and freshly ground pepper, to taste
    3 tablespoons water

Trim off and discard carrot ends; scrape carrots lightly to peel. In a skillet over medium heat, melt 4 tablespoons of the butter. Add carrots and sauté gently until golden on all sides. Sprinkle with onions, the 3 tablespoons parsley, thyme, oregano, sugar, wine, salt, and pepper; add the remaining butter and rapidly move pan back and forth over burner to mix ingredients. Reduce heat to low, add the water, cover tightly, and cook slowly until carrots are tender (about 25 minutes).

Serve carrots on a heated platter with pan juices poured over them. Garnish with parsley.

Serves 4 as a side dish

Potatoes Browned in Butter
Patates Tighanites

GGGGGGGGGGGGGGGGGGGGGGGGGGGGGGGGGG

Greeks love potatoes. Plan on two or three potatoes per person.

Small new potatoes, peeled
Butter
Salt and freshly ground pepper
Minced fresh oregano

Place potatoes in a saucepan, add water to cover, and bring to a boil. Boil potatoes until half-cooked (about 15 minutes); drain. Return potatoes to saucepan and place over low heat until potatoes are dry to the touch.

Melt butter in a heavy-bottomed skillet over medium heat; skillet should be thoroughly coated. Add potatoes and turn them to coat completely with butter. Season with salt and pepper and sprinkle generously with oregano. Brown potatoes on all sides, then reduce heat to low and cook until tender when pierced with a fork. Shake pan occasionally to prevent sticking and add more butter as needed.

Baked Variation Preheat oven to 350° F. Scrub potatoes but do not peel. Place potatoes in a double-thick sheet of aluminum foil large enough to enclose them completely. Bring up sides and ends to form a boat shape. For each 10 to 12 potatoes pour ¹/₂ cup chicken stock over the top, sprinkle with a little white wine, and dot with butter. Fold foil over potatoes and secure tightly. Place in a baking pan and bake until tender (about 1 hour). Alternatively, wrap in aluminum foil and cook on a grill over hot coals.

Mixed Greens Sauté
Horta Tighanita

GGGGGGGGGGGGGGGGGGGGGGGGGGGGGGGGGGGG

This is another popular way to cook mixed greens. Use any combination of fresh dandelion and mustard greens, broccoli raab, escarole, spinach, and Swiss chard. You will need to parboil the greens separately, to allow for the different cooking times. Prepare Garlic Sauce several hours in advance so that it is well chilled when served.

Garlic Sauce (see page 176)
2 to 3 pounds mixed greens
¹/₂ cup olive oil
1 clove garlic, minced
¹/₂ teaspoon each dried oregano and
*   thyme, crushed*
Salt and freshly ground pepper, to taste

Prepare Garlic Sauce and chill.

Wash greens in several changes of water to remove all dirt and sand. Bring a large pot filled with water to a boil. Add greens, one variety at a time, and parboil until half-cooked. Lift out with a slotted utensil and drain well.

When all of the greens are parboiled, place a large skillet over medium-high heat. Add oil, heat, and add garlic; sauté until translucent (about 3 minutes). Add greens and stir to coat with oil. Sprinkle with oregano, thyme, salt, and pepper; rapidly move pan back and forth over burner briefly, then cook over medium heat 10 minutes.

Transfer greens to a heated platter and serve Garlic Sauce on the side.

Serves 4 as a side dish

Boiled Greens with Lemon Juice and Olive Oil

Horta Vrasta

᠎᠎᠎᠎᠎᠎᠎᠎᠎᠎᠎᠎᠎᠎᠎᠎᠎᠎᠎᠎᠎᠎᠎᠎᠎᠎᠎᠎᠎᠎᠎᠎᠎᠎᠎᠎᠎

*F*or this classic recipe of the Greek vegetable repertoire, select greens according to what is fresh in the market. Try dandelion or mustard greens, broccoli raab, escarole, spinach, and Swiss chard, in any combination. Plan on about one-third pound greens per person.

> *Mixed greens of choice*
> *Salt, to taste*
> *Olive oil*
> *Freshly squeezed lemon juice*

Wash greens in several changes of water to remove all dirt and sand. Bring a large pot filled with water to a boil. Add salt. Immerse greens in the water and cook until tender. Most greens require about 10 minutes cooking. Dandelion greens take slightly longer and mustard greens even longer, so add these to the water first.

Remove greens from pot with a slotted utensil and transfer immediately to a serving bowl. They should be rather damp, so do not drain them too thoroughly. Drizzle with olive oil and lemon juice, or pass the oil and lemon juice at the table.

Celery Hearts in Egg-Lemon Sauce

Selino Avgolemono

᠎᠎᠎

*A*ny reputable Greek cook must master the classic egg-lemon sauce (avgolemono). Here it blankets tender poached celery hearts, in a superb vegetable dish that complements roasts or chops.

> *2 cups chicken stock*
> *6 celery hearts*
> *3 cups Egg-Lemon Sauce (see page 173)*

Pour stock in a saucepan and bring to a boil. Add celery hearts, cover, reduce heat, and simmer until tender but still firm (about 15 minutes). Remove with a slotted utensil to a heated platter and keep warm.

Prepare Egg-Lemon Sauce, using the stock in which celery hearts were cooked in place of the stock in the recipe. Spoon sauce over celery and serve immediately.

Serves 6 as a side dish

Variations For the celery hearts substitute either 1½ pounds broccoli, broken in florets; 12 medium leeks (including some green top), trimmed; 1½ pounds brussels sprouts; 1½ pounds asparagus, tough ends removed; or 6 artichokes, quartered and trimmed. Boil vegetable in salted water to cover until tender; drain and place on a heated platter. Prepare Egg-Lemon Sauce (using chicken stock in place of the vegetable cooking water). Spoon sauce over vegetable

Zucchini Fried in Olive Oil
Kolokithia Tighanita

This easy preparation is also ideal for artichokes and green beans (see variations). All of these vegetables are suitable accompaniments to grilled chops, roasted meats, or fried fish.

8 small zucchini (each about 5 in. long)
¼ cup olive oil
6 green onions, chopped
2 tablespoons minced fresh parsley, plus
    minced fresh parsley for garnish
1 clove garlic, minced
Pinch dried oregano, crushed
Salt and freshly ground pepper, to taste
3 tablespoons water

Trim off and discard zucchini ends; leave zucchini whole. In a skillet over medium heat, warm oil. Add zucchini and turn to coat with oil. Sprinkle with onions, the 2 tablespoons parsley, garlic, oregano, salt, and pepper; gently fry until lightly browned on all sides. Reduce heat to low, add the water, cover tightly, and cook slowly until zucchini are tender (about 20 minutes).

Serve zucchini on a heated platter with pan juices spooned over the top. Garnish with parsley.

Serves 4 as a side dish

Artichokes Variation Substitute 4 medium artichokes for zucchini. Fill a large pot with water and add juice of 1 lemon. Rinse artichokes under cold water and remove 3 or 4 outer layers of leaves. Slice 1 inch off leaf tops and trim stems. Cut artichokes in quarters lengthwise, remove thistles with a spoon, and drop quarters into the pot of water. Bring to a boil and cook 15 minutes; drain. To finish the dish, cook in a skillet with seasonings as directed in main recipe, but reduce cooking time to 15 minutes. Serve with pan juices.

Green Beans Variation Substitute 1½ pounds green beans for zucchini. Trim ends off green beans. Bring a saucepan of water to a boil, add beans, and parboil 5 minutes; drain. To finish the dish, cook in a skillet with seasonings as directed in main recipe, above, but reduce cooking time to 15 minutes. Serve with pan juices.

Cauliflower Fritters with Garlic Sauce
Krokettes Skordalia

Vegetable fritters are delicious as a side dish, an appetizer, or in a picnic lunch. For the fullest flavor fry the cauliflower in good-quality, fruity olive oil. Prepare Garlic Sauce several hours in advance to allow time for it to chill and for the flavors to blend.

Garlic Sauce (see page 176)
1 medium head (about 1 lb) cauliflower,
*   leaves removed and stem trimmed*
Flour, as needed for coating
2 or 3 egg yolks, for coating
Olive oil, as needed for deep-frying

Prepare Garlic Sauce and chill.

Bring a large pot of water to a boil. Add whole cauliflower and cook until tender but still firm (about 20 minutes). Drain and cool. Cut in half lengthwise, then cut crosswise in ½-inch-thick slices; pat slices dry with paper towels.

Spread flour on a plate. Put egg yolks in a small bowl and beat until blended. In a deep saucepan pour in oil to a depth of 4 inches. Heat until hot but not smoking. Dip cauliflower slices in flour and then in egg yolk. Slip into oil, taking care not to crowd the pan. Fry until golden brown (about 3 minutes), turning carefully to cook evenly. Remove with slotted utensil to paper towels to drain. Serve hot with Garlic Sauce.

Serves 4 as a side dish

Artichoke Fritters Variation Substitute 4 medium artichokes for cauliflower. Fill a large pot with water and add juice of 1 lemon. Rinse artichokes under cold water and remove 3 or 4 outer layers of leaves. Slice 1 inch off leaf tops and trim stems. Cut artichokes in quarters lengthwise, remove thistles with a spoon, and drop quarters into the pot of acidulated water. Bring to a boil and cook until almost tender (about 30 minutes). Drain, cool, and pat dry. Coat, deep-fry, and serve as directed in main recipe, above.

Eggplant Fritters Variation Substitute 1 medium-sized firm eggplant for cauliflower. Trim off and discard ends; cut eggplant crosswise in ½-inch-thick slices. Do not parboil. Coat, deep-fry, and serve as directed in main recipe, above.

Zucchini Fritters Variation Substitute 1½ pounds small zucchini for cauliflower. Trim off and discard ends; cut zucchini lengthwise in ½-inch-thick slices. Do not parboil. Coat, deep-fry, and serve as directed in main recipe, above.

Vegetable with Tomato Sauce
Lahanika me Saltsa Domata

ᎶᎶ

Greek villagers and city dwellers alike appreciate this simple preparation of a seasonal garden-fresh vegetable simmered in a quick-cooked tomato sauce.

2 cups Quick Tomato Sauce (see page 177)
Vegetable of choice (see below)

In a saucepan, bring tomato sauce to a simmer. Prepare vegetable as directed in following instructions, add to sauce, and cook until tender.

Serves 4 as a side dish

Artichokes   Rinse 4 medium artichokes under cold water and remove 3 or 4 outer layers of leaves. Slice 1 inch off leaf tops and trim stems. Cut artichokes in quarters lengthwise, remove thistles with a spoon, and drop quarters into sauce. Add juice of 1 lemon to sauce and simmer artichokes until tender (about 30 minutes).

Cauliflower   Cut 1 medium head (about 1 pound) cauliflower into florets and add to sauce. Add water, if needed, to cover cauliflower completely. Simmer until tender (15 to 20 minutes).

Eggplant   Peel and slice 1 medium (about 1 pound) eggplant. Season with salt and pepper and layer in tomato sauce. Simmer until very tender (about 30 minutes), adding water, if needed, to cover eggplant slices completely. Serve sprinkled with freshly grated *kefalotyri* or Parmesan cheese.

Green Beans   Trim ends from 1 pound green beans. Leave whole or cut on diagonal in 2-inch lengths. Parboil in boiling water to cover 5 minutes; drain, add to sauce, and simmer until tender (about 15 minutes).

Peas   Shell 2 to 3 pounds peas. Add peas to sauce and simmer until tender (10 to 15 minutes).

Potatoes   Peel and thickly slice 3 large potatoes. Add to sauce and simmer until tender (about 25 minutes).

Vegetables with White Sauce
Lahanika me Aspri Saltsa

╓╥╥╥

*F*or those who want to add an extra bit of rich-ness to this already luxuriously rich dish, sprinkle some crumbled feta over the top with the *kefalotyri* cheese.

> *2 pounds small zucchini, ends trimmed and halved lengthwise, or broccoli florets*
> *1½ to 2 cups Basic White Sauce (see page 174)*
> *Freshly grated kefalotyri or Parmesan cheese, for topping*

Preheat oven to 350° F. Bring a large pot filled with water to a boil. Add vegetable to water and cook until tender-crisp; drain well and transfer to a shallow baking dish. Add just enough white sauce to coat vegetable completely, turning vege-table in sauce to distribute sauce evenly.

Sprinkle top with cheese and bake until sauce is bubbly and lightly browned on top (about 10 minutes). Serve immediately.

Serves 6 as a side dish

Eggplant Variation Preheat broiler. Slice, coat, and fry 1 large eggplant according to directions in Eggplant Fritters Variation (see page 63). Com-bine with white sauce, sprinkle with kefalotyri, and slip under broiler until browned.

No-Bake Variation Coat boiled vegetable with white sauce as directed, but do not bake. Serve at once, sprinkled with grated cheese.

Rice and Noodles

*R*ice is central to Greek cuisine. It is stuffed into fowl, vegetables, or leaves; is made into a pudding; and is even added to the renowned *soupa avgolemono*. Most important, though, it is the basis of our pilafs, prepared plain or with seafood, meats, or vegetables.

Pasta appears less frequently on the Greek table than rice, but still plays an important role. Who dares speak of Greek cuisine without mentioning the classic noodle-and-meat casserole called *pastitsio?* My favorite of all the Greek noodle dishes, however, is the very simplest one: freshly cooked macaroni tossed with nutty browned butter and tangy *mizithra* cheese.

Rice and Fides Pilaf
Pilafi me Fides

*F*ides are dried, very thin noodles, similar to Italian vermicelli. They are commonly used in soups, but here are crushed into short lengths and then cooked with rice. Look for packaged fides in Greek delicatessens and well-stocked supermarkets.

  5 tablespoons butter
  1 cup crushed fides noodles
  1 cup long-grain white rice
  2 cups chicken stock, boiling
  Salt and freshly ground pepper, to taste

In a skillet over medium heat, melt butter. Add noodles and stir constantly until butter turns a light golden brown. Add rice, mix in well, then pour in stock. Stir briefly and season with salt and pepper. Cover, reduce heat to low, and cook until rice is tender and liquid is absorbed (about 20 minutes). Do not uncover pot during this time.

Remove from heat and let stand, covered, a few minutes. Uncover, fluff with a fork, and serve immediately.

Serves 4

Rice Pilaf
Pilafi

𝕘𝕘𝕘𝕘𝕘𝕘𝕘𝕘𝕘𝕘𝕘𝕘𝕘𝕘𝕘𝕘𝕘𝕘𝕘𝕘𝕘𝕘𝕘𝕘𝕘𝕘𝕘𝕘𝕘𝕘𝕘𝕘𝕘

*H*ere is a basic pilaf recipe that can be adapted to the dish it accompanies by preparing it with a complementary stock. For example, cook the rice in chicken stock for poultry entrées, clam juice for fish dishes, and beef stock for serving with beef or other red meats. Pan juices from roasting meats can also be used for part of the liquid. Just remember that the proportion of liquid to rice—2 parts liquid to 1 part rice—must remain constant.

4 cups water, stock, or pan juices
¼ cup butter
Salt, to taste
2 cups long-grain white rice

In a medium saucepan bring liquid to a boil. Add butter, salt, and rice; stir well. Cover, reduce heat to very low, and cook until rice is tender and liquid is absorbed (about 20 minutes).

Remove from heat and let stand, covered, a few minutes. Uncover, fluff with a fork, and serve immediately.

Serves 4 to 6

Rice with Tomato Sauce
Rizi Yahni

𝕘𝕘𝕘𝕘𝕘𝕘𝕘𝕘𝕘𝕘𝕘𝕘𝕘𝕘𝕘𝕘𝕘𝕘𝕘𝕘𝕘𝕘𝕘𝕘𝕘𝕘𝕘𝕘𝕘𝕘𝕘𝕘𝕘𝕘𝕘

*Y*ahni refers to a cooking method in which meats, vegetables, or grains are first sautéed with onions and seasonings in olive oil or butter and then simmered with water or stock and, usually, tomato sauce. Rice prepared in this manner complements roasted poultry or grilled lamb.

6 tablespoons butter
1 medium onion, finely chopped
1 clove garlic, minced
2 tablespoons minced fresh parsley
½ tablespoon minced fresh oregano or ½
*   teaspoon dried oregano, crushed*
1 bay leaf
1 cup Basic Tomato Sauce (see page 178)
½ cup dry white wine
1½ cups long-grain white rice
2 cups chicken stock, boiling
Salt and freshly ground pepper, to taste

In a saucepan over medium heat, melt 2 tablespoons of the butter. Add onion, garlic, and parsley; sauté until onion is translucent (about 5 minutes). Stir in oregano, bay leaf, tomato sauce, and wine, mixing well. Add the remaining butter and rice; sauté a few minutes. Pour in stock, season with salt and pepper, and bring to a boil. Cover, reduce heat to low, and cook until rice is tender and liquid is absorbed (about 20 minutes).

Remove from heat and let stand, covered, a few minutes. Uncover, fluff with a fork, and serve immediately.

Serves 4

Rice Pilaf with Mushrooms
Pilafi me Manitaria

*F*resh mushrooms cooked with white wine crown a fluffy, herb-laced pilaf. If you have an herb garden, create your own fines herbes blend for adding to the rice.

> ½ cup butter
> 2 medium onions, finely chopped
> ½ cup chopped fresh parsley
> 3 cloves garlic, minced
> 2 cups long-grain white rice
> 1 teaspoon dried fines herbes, crushed
> Salt, to taste
> 4 cups chicken stock, boiling
> 2 pounds fresh mushrooms, thinly sliced
> Freshly ground pepper, to taste
> 1 cup dry white wine

In a large, deep skillet over medium heat, melt ¼ cup of the butter. Add onions, parsley, and one third of the garlic and sauté until onions begin to soften (about 3 minutes). Add rice, sprinkle with fines herbes and salt, and sauté briefly. Pour in stock and stir well. Cover, reduce heat to low, and cook until rice is tender and liquid is absorbed (about 20 minutes). Remove from heat and let stand, covered, a few minutes.

While rice is cooking melt the remaining butter in a second skillet. Add mushrooms and the remaining garlic and cook over high heat until mushrooms are lightly browned (about 5 minutes). Season lightly with salt and pepper. Pour in wine, briefly move pan rapidly back and forth over burner, then cover and remove from heat.

To serve, spread rice on a heated platter. Spoon mushrooms with their pan juices evenly over the top.

Serves 8

Homemade Noodles
Spitisies Hilopite

If you have a pasta machine, use it for rolling out this egg-rich noodle dough. It will produce a very thin sheet of even thickness that can easily be cut into noodles of any width. In general Greeks prefer a wide noodle, much like the Italian *tagliatelle.* Use these fresh noodles for making Chicken With Homemade Noodles (see page 168); the eggy ribbons will absorb the flavor of the simmering tomato sauce. See Note for information on cooking or storing noodles.

2 cups flour, plus flour for board
1 teaspoon salt
2 whole eggs
4 egg yolks

Combine the 2 cups flour and salt in a sifter and sift into a large mixing bowl. Make a well in center of flour and break in whole eggs. Mix with your hands to combine, then add egg yolks; knead until dough is smooth and stiff. Divide dough in 3 equal portions.

On a lightly floured board, roll out 1 portion of dough into a large, paper-thin sheet. (Drape a tea towel over other dough portions to prevent them from drying out.) Roll out remaining dough portions in same manner. Let dough sheets stand, covered with tea towels, 20 to 30 minutes.

Uncover a dough sheet and roll up into a tight cylinder. Flatten top slightly and cut with a sharp knife crosswise in strips of desired width. Shake noodles loose so that they fall free. Transfer to a towel dusted with flour. Repeat with remaining dough sheets. Let noodles stand 5 to 10 minutes before cooking.

Makes about 1 3/4 pounds noodles

Note—To cook fresh noodles for dressing with a tomato-meat or other sauce, bring a large pot filled with water to a boil. Add salt to taste and drop in noodles. Cook until just tender to the bite, then drain. Dress with sauce of choice. This amount of noodles will serve 4 to 6.

To store fresh uncooked noodles, wrap in plastic wrap and refrigerate 2 to 3 days, or dry completely and store in a covered canister at room temperature.

Beef and Macaroni Casserole
Pastitsio

Every Greek taverna includes this hearty macaroni casserole on its menu. It is the lasagne of the Aegean, and indeed the original pastitsio was probably adapted from Italian cuisine. Although some prefer to make this dish with short macaroni shapes, I like to use long noodles. The thick Italian noodle called ziti may be substituted for Greek macaroni.

1/2 cup butter, plus butter for baking dish
1 onion, chopped
1 clove garlic, minced
1 tablespoon minced fresh parsley
2 pounds ground beef
1 teaspoon ground cinnamon, plus
*   cinnamon for garnish*
1/2 teaspoon freshly grated nutmeg
1/2 cup white wine
1 cup Basic Tomato Sauce (see page 178)
Salt and freshly ground pepper, to taste
4 cups Basic White Sauce (see page 174)
1 pound long macaroni noodles
3 eggs, lightly beaten
About 1 1/2 cups freshly grated kefalotyri
*   or Parmesan cheese*

In a large skillet over medium heat, melt 1/4 cup of the butter. Add onion, garlic, and parsley; sauté until onion is translucent (about 5 minutes). Add beef and sauté until lightly browned (about 5 minutes), breaking meat up with a fork as it cooks. Stir in the 1 teaspoon cinnamon, nutmeg, wine, tomato sauce, salt, and pepper; simmer, uncovered, 30 minutes, then remove from heat.

While meat mixture is cooking, prepare white sauce; set aside. Then bring a large pot of water to a boil. Add salt to taste and macaroni; cook according to package directions, or until just tender to the bite (about 15 minutes).

Meanwhile, melt the remaining 1/4 cup butter in a small saucepan. Drain macaroni and place in a large bowl. Add melted butter and eggs and toss to mix well. Add a generous sprinkling of cheese and toss again.

Preheat oven to 350° F. Butter a 9- by 13-inch baking dish. Spread half of the macaroni mixture in the bottom of the dish. Cover evenly with the meat sauce, sprinkle with some cheese, and then spread remaining macaroni over the top. Sprinkle again with cheese and pour reserved white sauce evenly over the top. Sprinkle lavishly with grated cheese and dust with a few pinches cinnamon.

Bake until nicely browned and set (about 1 hour). Cool slightly, then cut in squares to serve.

Serves 12 as an entrée

Athenian Macaroni

Makaronada

GGGGGGGGGGGGGGGGGGGGGGGGGGGGGGGG

Makaronada is the classic Greek macaroni dish, suitable for serving as a main course with a salad or as an accompaniment to meatballs or grilled chops. It is important that you use long macaroni noodles; short macaroni or broken noodles will not mix properly with the cheese and butter.

Salt, to taste
1 pound long macaroni noodles
About ¾ cup freshly grated mizithra,
    kefalotyri, or Parmesan cheese
½ cup butter

Bring a large pot of salted water to a boil. Add macaroni and cook according to package directions, or until just tender to the bite (about 15 minutes). Drain well.

Sprinkle a layer of cheese on a large platter. Cover with half the macaroni and sprinkle generously with more grated cheese. Cover with remaining macaroni and sprinkle again with cheese.

Melt butter in a large skillet over medium-high heat until it foams and turns golden brown; stir constantly with a wooden spoon so that it does not burn. Pour butter over macaroni and serve immediately.

Serves 4 as an entrée or 6 as a side dish

Macaroni with Meat Sauce
Makaronia Kima

This hearty noodle dish is a complete meal when served with a green salad.

¼ cup olive oil or butter
2 onions, finely chopped
3 cloves garlic, minced
2 pounds lean ground beef
¼ teaspoon ground cloves
½ teaspoon ground cinnamon
1 bay leaf
1 can (28 oz) plum tomatoes, chopped,
*   with their liquid*
3 tablespoons tomato paste
1 cup dry white wine
Salt, to taste
2 pounds long macaroni noodles
About 1½ cups freshly grated kefalotyri
*   or Parmesan cheese*
½ cup butter

In a large, deep skillet over medium-high heat, warm oil. Add onions and garlic and sauté until translucent (about 5 minutes). Add beef and brown well, breaking meat up with a fork as it cooks. Stir in cloves, cinnamon, bay leaf, tomatoes, tomato paste, and wine. Stir, reduce heat, and simmer until thick and flavors are well blended (about 1 hour). Adjust seasoning.

Bring a large pot of salted water to a boil. Add macaroni and cook according to package directions, or until just tender to the bite (15 to 20 minutes). Drain well.

Place half of the macaroni on a large heated platter. Sprinkle generously with cheese. Place remaining macaroni on top and sprinkle again with cheese.

Melt butter in a large skillet over medium-high heat until it foams and turns golden brown, stirring constantly with a wooden spoon so that it does not burn. Pour butter over macaroni, then spoon some of the meat sauce over the top.

Serve macaroni with remaining meat sauce in a bowl alongside. Pass additional grated cheese and serve immediately.

Serves 8 as an entrée

Sweets and Breads

To discover the sweets of Greece, follow the scent of almonds and honey; of cinnamon, nutmeg, and cloves; of orange flower water and rose petals. Such heavenly bites are enjoyed throughout the day and into the night, for Greeks eat sweets whenever the mood strikes. In midmorning the staff of a *zacharoplasteion* ("sweet shop") may be serving up batches of fresh *loukoumades* ("honey puffs"); late in the evening the same shop will be crowded with people eating diamonds of honey-sweetened baklava and drinking cups of strong, thick coffee.

The many holy days of the Greek Orthodox calendar are traditionally celebrated with special cookies and breads. At Christmastime ovens are stacked with brandy-laced shortbread cookies called *kourabiedes*; for Easter Sunday bracelet-shaped *koulourakia* are baked. Every day of the year brings delicate filo pastry concealing a silky custard, cups of creamy rice pudding, or syrupy preserved fruits, known as *spoon sweets*.

Custards, Puddings, and Confections

The Greeks eat custards and puddings as both snacks and desserts. A bowl of *rizogalo* ("rice pudding") sometimes even appears on the breakfast table. These sweets, along with such confections as halvah, are not as elaborate as many of the Greek pastries and breads, but they are consumed with great enthusiasm nonetheless.

Orange-Scented Custard
Galatopeta

GGGGGGGGGGGGGGGGGGGGGGGGGGGGGGGGGGGGGGGGGGGGGGGGGGGGGGGGGGGGGGGGGGGGGGGGGGGGGGGG

*E*laborate meals in ancient Greece were usually concluded with fresh fruits and an assortment of cheesecakes, perhaps the forerunners of today's smooth, rich *galatopeta*.

4 cups milk
1¾ cups sugar
¾ cup farina
1 cup unsalted butter, plus butter for
*   baking dish*
1 teaspoon vanilla extract
2 teaspoons freshly grated orange zest
2 tablespoons orange- or peach-flavored
*   liqueur*
10 eggs, separated
Spiced Syrup (see following recipe)
Ground cinnamon, for garnish

Preheat oven to 350° F. In a large saucepan over low heat, combine milk and one half of the sugar, stirring to dissolve sugar. Slowly add farina, stirring constantly with a wooden spoon until mixture thickens and is smooth. Add the 1 cup butter and stir over low heat until completely blended into milk mixture. Remove from heat and add vanilla, orange zest, and liqueur. Stir well and cool to room temperature.

In a large mixing bowl, combine egg yolks and the remaining sugar and beat with a rotary beater or an electric beater until frothy. In a second bowl beat egg whites until stiff peaks form; gently fold whites into yolks. Add cooled milk mixture and stir well.

Butter a 9- by 13-inch baking dish and pour batter into it. Bake until firm and a knife inserted in center comes out clean (about 35 minutes).

While custard is baking, prepare Spiced Syrup. Remove custard from oven and sprinkle lightly with cinnamon. Let cool to room temperature and cut in 2-inch squares. Serve with Spiced Syrup on the side.

Makes about 2 dozen squares

Spiced Syrup
1 cup water
1½ cups sugar
3 whole cloves
1 cinnamon stick (about 2 in. long)
2 teaspoons freshly grated orange zest
1 teaspoon vanilla extract
2 tablespoons orange- or peach-flavored
*   liqueur*

In a small saucepan over medium heat, combine the water, sugar, cloves, cinnamon stick, and orange zest. Bring to a boil, stirring to dissolve sugar. Reduce heat and simmer 15 minutes. Remove from heat and stir in vanilla and liqueur. Cool to room temperature.

Custard with Filo

Galatoboureko

When friends come for an afternoon visit, Greek hosts will serve a luscious sweet, such as this pastry-wrapped custard, and demitasses of strong coffee. *Galatoboureko* is best when made a day in advance so that the syrup has time to infuse the many pastry layers. Read the information on working with filo dough (see page 14) before beginning the recipe.

> *Orange-Scented Custard (see page 74)*
> *Spiced Syrup (see page 74)*
> *About 1 pound unsalted butter, melted and cooled*
> *1 pound filo dough, thawed overnight in refrigerator if frozen*

Prepare custard and syrup; let both cool.
Preheat oven to 350° F. Brush a 9- by 13-inch baking dish with melted butter. Unfold filo dough so it lays flat, then cover to prevent it from drying out. Line dish with 10 to 12 filo sheets, brushing each with melted butter before adding the next sheet. Pour cooled custard on top of filo and spread evenly with a spatula. Cover with the remaining filo sheets, brushing each with butter as you layer it in the dish. Lavishly brush the top sheet with butter. With a sharp knife or single-edged razor blade, cut in 3-inch squares, going only deep enough to reach through the unfilled top filo layers.

Bake until golden and custard is set (45 minutes to 1 hour). Remove from oven and cool slightly. Slowly pour cooled syrup evenly over the top; the syrup should saturate the filo and custard thoroughly. Cool several hours or overnight. Finish cutting through the filo layers to serve.

Serves 12

Custard Filo Rolls

Preheat oven to 350° F. Prepare custard and syrup; let cool. Cut filo sheets in half crosswise. Brush each half sheet with melted butter, then fold in half to form a square. Place 1 tablespoon custard near lower right-hand corner of square, fold corner over filling, and then fold sides over filling. Roll up like a jelly roll.

Form rolls with remaining custard and filo. Arrange rolls, seam side down, in buttered baking dish. Brush tops with melted butter and bake until golden and filling is set (about 30 minutes). Remove rolls from oven and pour cooled syrup over them. Cool several hours or overnight.

Athenian Rice Pudding
Rizogalo

Some of the smaller food shops in Athens sell just a few specialty items such as this cinnamon-dusted rice pudding.

4 cups milk
½ cup water
½ cup short-grain white rice
Pinch salt
4 egg yolks
¾ cup sugar
Zest of 1 small orange or
*   1 lemon, or a combination*
1 teaspoon vanilla extract
Ground cinnamon, for garnish
Whipping cream (optional)

Pour milk into a saucepan, place over low heat, and heat until small bubbles form at edge of pan. Meanwhile, heat the water in a small pan, add rice and salt, and parboil 5 minutes; drain.

Add drained rice to milk and cook over low heat, stirring occasionally, until rice is very tender and mixture is thick (about 45 minutes).

In a small bowl beat egg yolks with sugar until ribbony. Remove rice-milk mixture from heat. Beat about 1 cup of the milk mixture into the egg yolks, then add to saucepan, beating continuously until well blended. Add citrus zest, return saucepan to low heat, and cook, stirring constantly, until creamy and thick (about 5 minutes). Mix in vanilla and divide among 6 bowls.

Sprinkle tops with cinnamon and cool to room temperature. Offer whipped cream at table.

Serves 6

Grape Must Pudding
Moustoalevria

During the grape harvest in Greece, some of the wine must is used to make this pudding. My recipe calls for commercial grape juice, which produces excellent results.

2 cups unsweetened grape juice
2 tablespoons each sugar and cornstarch
Dash each ground cloves and cinnamon
¼ teaspoon anise extract
Whole blanched almonds or chopped
*   walnuts, for garnish*

Pour all but 2 tablespoons of the grape juice into a saucepan over medium heat. Add sugar and bring to a gentle boil, stirring to dissolve sugar. Dissolve cornstarch in reserved 2 tablespoons grape juice and stir into pan, mixing thoroughly.

Add cloves, cinnamon, and anise extract and continue stirring until mixture comes to a full boil and thickens (about 2 minutes). Remove from heat and divide among 4 dessert bowls. Cool to room temperature and garnish with nuts.

Serves 4

Baked Halvah

Halvah tou Fournou

What goes into the confection known as *halvah* varies from season to season and cook to cook. Most often farina or rice flour is mixed with butter, sugar, milk, and sometimes nuts and dried fruits. This recipe yields a very rich baked halvah, drizzled with a brandy-flavored syrup. During the Lenten period, a simpler halvah, made from only farina, oil, and sugar, is served.

*Brandied Sugar Syrup (see following
    recipe)*
*1 cup unsalted butter, softened, plus
    butter for baking dish*
1 cup sugar
6 eggs
2 cups farina
*1 teaspoon each baking powder and
    ground cinnamon*
1 teaspoon vanilla extract
1 cup pine nuts

Prepare syrup; cool to room temperature.

In a large bowl beat the 1 cup butter with a wooden spoon until creamy. Add sugar and beat until smooth; set aside.

Preheat oven to 350° F. Break eggs, separating whites into a large bowl and yolks into a smaller bowl. Beat yolks until pale yellow. Beat egg whites until stiff peaks form, then fold in yolks. Stir farina into butter mixture, then beat in eggs. Stir in baking powder, cinnamon, vanilla, and pine nuts, beating to mix thoroughly.

Butter a 9- by 13-inch baking dish and pour in halvah mixture, smoothing top with a spatula. Bake until set (about 35 minutes).

Remove halvah from oven and pour cooled syrup evenly over top. Cool to room temperature. Cut into small diamonds or squares to serve.

Makes about 3 dozen pieces

Brandied Sugar Syrup

2 cups sugar
3 cups water
1 whole clove
3 tablespoons brandy

In a saucepan over medium-high heat, combine sugar, the water, and clove. Bring to a boil, stirring to dissolve sugar. Reduce heat and simmer 10 minutes, stirring occasionally. Remove from heat, stir in brandy, and cool to room temperature.

Orange-Almond Crêpes

Tighanites Yemistes

You will need to let the crêpe batter chill for several hours before assembling this elegant dessert. The almond-scented orange filling will also need time to cool before it can be spooned onto the delicate pancakes. Metaxa, a full-bodied brandy excellent for sipping and cooking, can be found in Greek markets.

Crêpes (see following page)
2 oranges
1 cup sugar
1 cup water
1 slice lemon
1 small stick cinnamon (about 1 in. long)
Dash freshly grated vanilla bean or
  ¼ teaspoon vanilla extract
2 tablespoons almond-flavored liqueur
3 tablespoons slivered blanched almonds
½ cup unsalted butter
Dash freshly squeezed lemon juice
¼ cup orange-flavored liqueur
¼ cup Metaxa brandy

Prepare crêpes; cool, stack, and set aside.

Following directions for Orange Spoon Sweet (see page 87), grate and section the rinds of the 2 oranges, then string rinds and parboil in water. Following the third boiling, remove and carefully slice rinds very thinly. Set aside.

In a saucepan combine sugar, the water, lemon slice, cinnamon, vanilla, and almond liqueur; bring to a boil and skim off any foam that forms on top. Add sliced orange rinds and almonds to syrup, reduce heat, and simmer 5 minutes. Remove from heat and lift out and discard lemon slice and cinnamon stick. Let cool.

Place a heaping tablespoonful of cooled orange mixture in center of each crêpe, then overlap sides to cover filling.

In a chafing dish or large, shallow pan over medium-low heat, melt butter. Add lemon juice and orange-flavored liqueur and stir into butter to mix well. Place filled crêpes in pan, seam side down, and continuously spoon butter mixture over them until well heated. Pour Metaxa over warmed crêpes and carefully ignite with a long match, shaking pan to distribute sauce evenly.

When flames subside, transfer crêpes to heated individual serving plates. Spoon some of the sauce over each serving.

Serves 8

Continued—

Orange-Almond Crêpes—continued

Crêpes

2 cups sifted flour
4 eggs
1 cup each water and milk
¼ cup unsalted butter, melted and cooled, plus unsalted butter for cooking
Dash orange flower water
1 teaspoon sugar

Place flour in a large mixing bowl. With a whisk, slowly blend in eggs until well mixed. Gradually stir in the water and milk. Add the ¼ cup butter, orange flower water, and sugar; whisk vigorously until batter is smooth. Pour through a sieve to remove lumps; cover and chill several hours.

Place a 5- or 6-inch crêpe pan or small, heavy skillet over medium heat. Melt a small dab of butter, then wipe out excess with a paper towel. Quickly whisk chilled batter. Remove pan from heat and add just enough batter to pan to coat thinly, tilting pan so that batter evenly covers bottom. Return to heat and cook until lightly browned on bottom (about 1 minute). Turn and cook second side until lightly browned (about 45 seconds). Remove to a plate to cool completely, then stack until ready to use. Repeat with remaining batter.

Makes 16 to 20 crêpes

Farina Diamonds

Halvah

This is another type of halvah, one that is cooked on the stove-top, then poured into a pan and cooled to a marvelously fudgy consistency. The walnuts add an interesting contrast in texture and flavor.

4 cups milk
2 cups sugar
½ cup unsalted butter, plus butter for baking dish
1 cup farina
1 teaspoon ground cinnamon
About 36 walnut halves

In a saucepan over low heat, bring milk to a boil. Add sugar and cook, stirring to dissolve sugar, 5 minutes. Remove from heat.

In a heavy skillet over low heat, melt the ½ cup butter. Slowly add farina and cook over low heat, stirring constantly, until farina is golden brown (10 to 15 minutes). Gradually add milk mixture to farina and stir continuously until mixture is consistency of thick porridge (about 10 minutes).

Butter a 9- by 13-inch baking dish and pour mixture into dish. Sprinkle top with cinnamon and let cool. Cut in small diamond shapes and press a walnut half on top of each diamond.

Makes about 3 dozen diamonds

*E*ach Greek family has its own treasure trove of sweets recipes, detailed instructions handed down from generation to generation. They range from many-layered filo pastries to delicate cookies. Some are time-consuming to prepare, but the delicious results are worth the effort.

Walnut Cake

Karidopeta

*A*s early as the fourth century B.C., Greeks were cultivating walnuts and pressing them for their flavorful oil. Today walnuts appear in many of their best-known sweets, among them this cake redolent of cinnamon and orange.

Cinnamon Sugar Syrup (see following recipe)
1 cup unsalted butter, softened, plus butter for baking dish
1 cup sugar
6 eggs
1 cup flour, sifted
1 cup farina
2½ teaspoons baking powder
1 teaspoon ground cinnamon
1 teaspoon freshly grated orange zest
1 cup finely chopped walnuts

Prepare syrup and set aside to cool.

Preheat oven to 350° F. In a large mixing bowl, cream together the 1 cup butter and sugar with a wooden spoon until light and fluffy. Add eggs, one at a time, beating continuously. Beat in flour, farina, baking powder, cinnamon, and orange zest. Mix in walnuts.

Butter a 9- by 13-inch baking dish and pour batter into it. Bake until a knife blade inserted in center comes out clean (about 30 minutes).

Remove cake from oven and immediately pour cooled syrup evenly over top. Cool to room temperature and cut in small diamond shapes to serve.

Makes about 3 dozen diamonds

Cinnamon Sugar Syrup

3 cups water
2 cups sugar
1 cinnamon stick (about 2 in. long)
1 slice lemon
¼ cup rum (optional)

In a medium saucepan over medium heat, combine all ingredients. Bring to a boil, stirring to dissolve sugar. Cook rapidly 20 minutes. Remove from heat and cool to room temperature.

Nut-and-Honey-Filled Filo Pastry
Baklava

Some form of baklava is found throughout the Middle East. In Greece the buttery pastry layers are lined with pine nuts, walnuts, almonds, pistachios, or even a crumbled cookie mixture. Whatever the filling, the baklava is traditionally drenched with streams of honey from Hymettus, an area near Athens where bees feed on sweet fig blossoms. Read the tips on working with filo dough (see page 14) before beginning the recipe.

1 pound (about 2 cups) shelled walnuts
*   (2 lb unshelled)*
1 pound blanched almonds
2 teaspoons ground cinnamon
1 teaspoon ground allspice
⅔ cup sugar
1 pound unsalted butter, melted and
*   cooled*
1 pound filo dough, thawed in
*   refrigerator overnight if frozen*
About 3 dozen whole cloves
Sugar syrup (see following recipe)

Preheat oven to 350° F. Coarsely grind (or finely chop) walnuts and almonds; place in a mixing bowl. Add cinnamon, allspice, and sugar; mix thoroughly.

Brush a 9- by 13-inch baking dish with melted butter. Unfold filo dough so it lays flat, then cover to prevent it from drying out. Line dish with 10 to 12 filo sheets, brushing each with melted butter before adding the next sheet. Spread a thin layer of the nut mixture over the filo, cover with a filo sheet, brush with butter, and cover with another thin layer of the nut mixture. Repeat process until all of the nut mixture is used. Then cover with the remaining filo sheets, brushing each with butter as you layer it in the dish. Brush top sheet lavishly with butter.

With a very sharp knife or single-edged razor blade, cut diagonally across the pan to make small diamonds, going only deep enough to reach through the unfilled top filo layers. Insert a clove up to base of bud in center of each diamond.

Bake until evenly browned and crispy (about 1½ hours). Meanwhile, prepare syrup and set aside to cool.

Remove pastry from oven, cool slightly, and pour cooled syrup evenly over the top; it should penetrate all of the layers. Cool several hours or overnight. Finish cutting through the filo layers to serve.

Makes about 3 dozen diamonds

Sugar Syrup
2 cups honey
2 cups water
2 cups sugar
2 cinnamon sticks (each about 2 in. long)
1 teaspoon freshly grated orange zest
1 teaspoon vanilla extract

In a small saucepan over medium heat, combine all ingredients. Bring to a boil, stirring to dissolve sugar. Reduce heat and simmer 10 minutes. Strain and cool to room temperature.

Honey Rolls

Diples

Ideally, these honey-drizzled pastries are served within moments of being cooked. Do not despair if making the first batch is tedious work and the rolls are not perfectly cylindrical; forming them takes patience and practice. When you taste the result, you will be compensated.

6 eggs
3 cups flour, sifted, plus flour as needed
1/2 teaspoon each baking powder
   and salt
1/2 cup butter, melted and cooled
High-quality vegetable oil, for deep-
   frying
Honey, to taste
Ground cinnamon, to taste
Finely chopped walnuts or pistachios
   (optional)

Break eggs into a large mixing bowl and beat with a rotary or electric beater until very light. Combine the 3 cups flour, baking powder, and salt in a sifter and sift into eggs. With your hands, work dry ingredients into eggs to make a smooth consistency that does not stick to your fingers. Add flour as needed to eliminate stickiness.

Transfer dough to a lightly floured board. Add butter, a few drops at a time, and knead until dough is smooth (about 10 minutes). Pull off about a quarter of the dough and cover remaining dough with a tea towel to prevent it from drying out. With a rolling pin, roll out dough paper-thin. Cut in 4- by 6-inch rectangles and sprinkle lightly with flour. Cover rectangles and repeat with remaining dough.

In a saucepan pour oil to a depth of about 3 inches and heat oil to 360° F. While oil is heating, pour some honey into a small saucepan and place over very low heat to warm.

Drop rectangles, one at a time, into oil; as each enters the oil, use 2 forks to roll it up quickly into a cylinder. Fry rolls until lightly golden on all sides; remove to paper towels to drain, then arrange side by side on a large serving platter. Drizzle lavishly with honey and sprinkle with cinnamon and nuts.

Makes about 4 dozen rolls

Honey Puffs
Loukoumades

GGGGGGGGGGGGGGGGGGGGGGGGGGGGGGGGGGGGGGGGGGGGGGGGGGGGGGGGGGGGGGGGGGGGGGGG

*O*f all the Greek sweets, *loukoumades* evoke the most vivid memories of moonlit nights and midnight parties under Athenian skies. Both children and adults recall the mounds of golden puffs drizzled with honey and dusted with our ever-present cinnamon.

2 packages active dry yeast
½ cup warm (105° to 115° F) water
1 cup warm (105° to 115° F) milk
¼ cup sugar
1 teaspoon salt
2 eggs, lightly beaten
½ cup butter, melted and cooled
3 to 4 cups sifted flour
High-quality vegetable oil, for deep-frying
About 1 cup honey, or to taste
Ground cinnamon, to taste

In a small bowl sprinkle yeast over the warm water and let stand to soften (about 5 minutes). Meanwhile, pour milk into a large bowl and add sugar and salt. Stir in yeast mixture and eggs; add butter and beat well. Slowly add 3 cups flour, beating continuously until batter is smooth, sticky, and thick. Add more flour as needed to arrive at correct consistency. Cover bowl with a tea towel and let dough rise in a warm place until doubled in bulk (2 to 3 hours).

In a medium saucepan pour oil to a depth of 3 or 4 inches and heat to 360° F. While oil is heating, pour some honey into a small saucepan and place over very low heat to warm.

Stir batter well. Drop batter from a tablespoon into hot oil and cook, turning spoonfuls in oil, until batter puffs and is golden brown on all sides (about 2 minutes). Remove with a slotted utensil to paper towels to drain briefly, then arrange a layer of the puffs on a platter. Drizzle with warm honey, dust with cinnamon, and top with a second layer of puffs. Continue in this manner until all the puffs are layered and dressed. Serve at once.

Makes about 3 dozen puffs

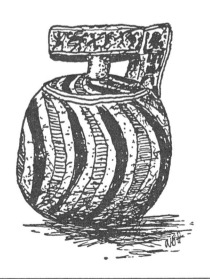

Clove Cookies
Kourabiedes

Christmas celebrations always include these buttery cookies, each studded with a whole clove and dressed in a ruffled paper cup.

1 cup unsalted butter, softened
½ cup sifted confectioners' sugar, plus confectioners' sugar for garnish
1 egg yolk
½ teaspoon each vanilla extract and almond extract
1 tablespoon brandy
2½ cups sifted pastry flour, plus flour for board
About 4 dozen whole cloves

Place butter in a mixing bowl and whip with an electric mixer until white and very fluffy (about 25 minutes). Add the ½ cup sugar, egg yolk, vanilla and almond extracts, and brandy; beat well with mixer. Add the 2½ cups flour and beat until dough is easy to handle. Turn onto a floured board and knead until dough forms a soft ball (3 to 4 minutes).

Preheat oven to 350° F. Shape dough into walnut-sized balls and place on an ungreased baking sheet. Insert a clove up to bud base in center of each ball. Bake until lightly golden (15 to 20 minutes).

While cookies are baking sift sugar on a large sheet of waxed paper. With a spatula remove cookies to waxed paper and sift more sugar over top; roll lightly to coat cookies completely, then cool. Transfer each ball to a paper cupcake liner and sift more sugar over top.

Makes about 4 dozen cookies

Almond Variation After mixing in flour, add to batter ½ cup almonds, lightly toasted and ground.

Sesame-Topped Butter Cookies
Koulourakia

These cookies are an Easter tradition but are good any time of the year, at any time of the day. Try dunking them in your morning coffee.

1 cup unsalted butter, softened
2 cups sugar
6 whole eggs, lightly beaten, plus 2 egg
  yolks, lightly beaten, for glaze
½ cup milk
8 to 9 cups sifted flour
4 teaspoons baking powder
½ teaspoon each ground cinnamon and
  allspice
1 teaspoon vanilla extract
3 tablespoons anise-flavored liqueur
⅓ cup sesame seed

In a large mixing bowl, beat butter with a wooden spoon until soft and creamy; add sugar and beat thoroughly. Mix in whole beaten eggs and then milk.

Combine 8 cups flour and baking powder in a sifter and sift into egg mixture. Beat thoroughly, then add cinnamon, allspice, vanilla, and liqueur; mix again.

Preheat oven to 350° F. Turn dough onto a lightly floured board and knead until firm and smooth, adding more flour as needed. To test for correct consistency, roll a ball of dough in your hand; it should feel firm and not at all sticky. Pull off a small piece of dough and roll into a rope 3 inches long and ½ inch in diameter. Bring ends of rope around to meet, forming a circle; press ends together with your fingertips. Brush circle with egg yolk, dip in sesame seed, and place on a baking sheet. Repeat with remaining dough.

Bake until very lightly browned (about 15 minutes). Remove to wire racks to cool.

Makes about 5 dozen cookies

Spoon Sweets

Glyka koutaliou (spoon sweets) bring back memories of my childhood. One of the first things a young girl learns is how to prepare the tray that is presented to an afternoon guest. The tray holds an elegant cut-glass compote filled with an array of delectable preserves, a small glass of water with a spoon laying across the top of it, and a demitasse of coffee and/or a pony of ouzo or brandy.

The guest dips the spoon in one of the spoon sweets, eats it, and stirs whatever syrup still adheres to the spoon into the water. Then the sweetened water is drunk, followed by the coffee, ouzo, or brandy. Here are recipes for classic spoon sweets. They are also delicious on muffins and biscuits.

Orange Spoon Sweet
Portokali Glyko

᎒᎒᎒

*F*or this preserve you will simmer a necklace of orange rinds until beautifully glazed, then break the strand and store the sweet pieces in syrup.

> *2 large oranges*
> *1 cup sugar*
> *1 cup water*
> *1 slice lemon*

Lightly grate whole oranges until their surfaces are smooth and no longer shiny (do not grate away the color). With a sharp knife cut through rind just to fruit to form 8 vertical sections from each orange. Remove rind from each section, then cut away any white membrane from rind. Roll up each piece of rind into a coil and, with a needle and heavy thread, string coils to form a necklace-like strand. Tie ends of the thread together. Reserve orange pulp for another use.

Place strand in a saucepan, add water to cover, and bring to a boil. Drain, repeat procedure, and drain again. Fill the pan with water a third time, bring to a boil, and boil until rinds are tender when pierced with a knife. Drain and dry thoroughly with paper towels.

In a saucepan over medium heat, combine sugar, the water, and lemon slice. Bring to a boil, stirring; remove any foam that forms on surface. Add string of rinds and simmer until a very thick syrup is formed (30 to 45 minutes). Remove from heat and cool.

Discard lemon slice. Lift rind necklace from syrup and remove and discard string. Place rinds in 1 or 2 sterilized jars and add syrup to cover. Cover and store at room temperature.

Makes about 1 pint

Grapefruit Spoon Sweet (Cytro Glyko) Substitute 2 thick-skinned grapefruits for the oranges. Prepare in the same manner as Orange Spoon Sweet, but add 1½ tablespoons freshly squeezed lemon juice to the sugar-water mixture in place of the lemon slice.

Quince-Almond Spoon Sweet
Kythoni me Amygthala Glyko

᎒᎒᎒᎒᎒᎒᎒᎒᎒᎒᎒᎒᎒᎒᎒᎒᎒᎒᎒᎒᎒᎒᎒᎒᎒᎒᎒᎒᎒᎒

*P*lan on making this delectable sweet in the fall, when large golden quinces appear in the market or on a backyard tree.

1 pound quinces
2 fresh geranium leaves
¾ cup water
2 cups sugar
2 sticks cinnamon (each about
*   2 in. long)*
1 whole clove
½ cup whole blanched almonds
Juice of 1 lemon

Peel and core quinces; coarsely grate pulp. Combine quince and geranium leaves in a saucepan with the water; bring to a boil and simmer until quince is tender (about 10 minutes).

Gradually add sugar, stirring constantly. Add cinnamon, clove, and almonds. Bring to a boil, then reduce heat slightly. Simmer, stirring occasionally and skimming away any foam that forms on top, until a thick syrup is formed that coats the back of a metal spoon (45 minutes to 1 hour). Stir in lemon juice, simmer briefly, and remove from heat.

Remove and discard cinnamon and clove. Cool, pour into sterilized jars, cover, and store at room temperature.

Makes about 1 pint

Rose-Petal Spoon Sweet
Triantafillo Glyko

᎒᎒᎒᎒᎒᎒᎒᎒᎒᎒᎒᎒᎒᎒᎒᎒᎒᎒᎒᎒᎒᎒᎒᎒᎒᎒᎒᎒᎒᎒᎒᎒᎒᎒

*T*he most highly prized rose-petal preserves in Greece come from the island of Chios, in the eastern Aegean. For the fullest flavor, select deep-colored, fragrant red roses.

4 cups fresh red rose petals (from about
*   12 roses)*
2 cups water
2 cups sugar
1 tablespoon freshly squeezed lemon
*   juice*

Remove base end of rose petals, wash petals gently, and drain.

In a saucepan over medium heat, combine the water, 1 cup of the sugar, and lemon juice; bring to a boil, stirring to dissolve sugar. Gently add rose petals to syrup; boil for a few minutes, then slowly mix in the remaining sugar, stirring until dissolved. Bring to a full boil, reduce heat slightly, and simmer until syrup forms a ball when dropped from tip of spoon onto a saucer (45 minutes to 1 hour).

Skim away any foam on surface and cool. Pour into sterilized jars, cover, and store at room temperature.

Makes about 2 pints

We Greeks are so fond of sweets that even many of our breads, especially the renowned Easter *lambropsomo* and New Year's Day *vasilopeta,* are cakelike in taste and texture. When the loaves are cut, the fragrance of spices fills the air.

Easter Bread

Lambropsomo

Dyed-red eggs, positioned to mark the points of the Greek Orthodox cross, decorate this traditional Easter loaf. The bread should be baked in a large round pan about 12 inches in diameter and 2 inches deep. Any remaining dough is baked in small loaves and given away as gifts. Note that dough needs to rise about six hours total.

1 teaspoon ground allspice
1½ teaspoons anise
1 cup cold water
4 packages active dry yeast
1 cup warm (105° to 115° F) water
16 to 18 cups flour (4 to 4½ lb), plus
    flour for board and pans
1 teaspoon salt
10 whole eggs, lightly beaten, plus 3 egg
    yolks, beaten, for glaze
2½ cups sugar

1 cup unsalted butter, melted and
    cooled, plus melted butter for brushing
    bowl, dough, and pans
1½ cups milk
5 hard-cooked eggs, dyed red, for large
    loaf, plus additional eggs as needed
    for smaller loaves
⅓ cup sesame seed

In a small saucepan combine allspice, anise, and the cold water. Bring to a boil and boil a few minutes until water takes on the flavors of the spices; strain, reserving liquid, and set aside.

In a small bowl sprinkle yeast over the warm water and let stand to soften (about 5 minutes). Combine 16 cups flour and salt in a large sifter and sift into a large mixing bowl. Make a well in center of flour. In a medium bowl beat whole eggs with sugar until blended. Pour into flour well the yeast mixture, egg-sugar mixture, the 1 cup

Continued—

melted butter, milk, and reserved spice liquid and mix with hands until all ingredients are thoroughly blended. Add more flour as needed to form a smooth dough.

Turn dough onto a lightly floured board and knead until firm, smooth, elastic, and not sticky (about 10 minutes). Butter a large bowl. Form dough into a ball and place in buttered bowl. Brush top of dough with butter, cover bowl with a tea towel, and set in warm place to rise until doubled in bulk (1 to 1½ hours).

Punch down dough, turn onto a floured board, and knead gently until smooth. Return to greased bowl, brush top of dough with butter, and re-cover with towel. Set in warm place to rise again until doubled in bulk (about 1 hour). Repeat kneading and rising process one more time.

Butter a shallow, round pan about 12 inches in diameter. Punch down dough and form two thirds of it into a round loaf; place in prepared pan. Make a shallow depression in center of loaf and then 4 additional depressions at opposite edges of loaf, to mark the points of a cross. Place a dyed egg in each depression. Set aside a small portion of the remaining dough for decorating loaf.

Divide remaining dough into as many small loaves as desired. Butter as many small round pans as necessary, form dough into small round loaves, and place in pans. Press 1 dyed egg into each small loaf, if desired. Cover all of the pans (and small portion of reserved dough) with tea towels and set in warm place to rise until almost doubled in bulk (2 to 3 hours).

Preheat oven to 350° F. On a lightly floured board roll out reserved dough into a thin sheet. Cut in 10 narrow strips, each about 1 inch longer than the length of an egg. Make a cross on top of each egg with 2 strips, pressing ends of strips into loaf to secure the eggs in place. Brush crosses and surface of loaf with egg yolk. Sprinkle generously with sesame seed. Brush small loaves with egg yolk and sprinkle with sesame seed.

Bake loaves until golden brown and knife blade inserted in center comes out clean (50 to 60 minutes for large loaf, 35 to 40 minutes for smaller loaves, depending upon size). Transfer to wire racks to cool.

Makes 1 large and several small loaves

Easter Twists (Tsoureki) Prepare dough through third rising as directed in main recipe. Omit dyed eggs. Preheat oven to 350° F. Divide dough into 9 equal portions and roll each portion into a narrow rope about 20 inches long. Place 3 ropes side by side on a lightly floured board and press them together at one end. Braid strands, being careful not to stretch the dough as you work. Pinch ends together at lower end and bring lower end around to top end to form a wreath. Repeat with remaining strands, forming 3 wreaths in all. Place on buttered baking sheets, brush with egg yolk, and sprinkle with sesame seed. Bake until golden brown (about 45 minutes). Transfer to wire racks to cool.

Makes 3 large twisted bread rings

New Year's Bread

Vasilopeta

A special ceremony accompanies the serving of this holiday bread, in which a silver or gold coin has been baked. The head of the house cuts the loaf at midnight on New Year's Eve; the family member who is lucky enough to find the coin in a slice is blessed with good fortune for the coming year. It is customary to bake a single, large loaf of this cakelike bread, but the dough may be divided in half to form two smaller loaves. Wrap leftover bread and store at room temperature; toast slices for a morning treat. Note that the dough needs to rise for three hours.

2 packages active dry yeast
½ cup warm (105° to 115° F) water
5 to 6 cups flour, plus flour for board
½ cup warm (105° to 115° F) milk
1 cup unsalted butter, melted and
    cooled, plus melted butter for brushing
    bowl, dough, and baking sheet
6 whole eggs, lightly beaten, plus 1 or 2
    egg yolks, beaten, for glaze
2 cups sugar
½ teaspoon each salt and freshly grated
    nutmeg
1 teaspoon ground cinnamon
1 tablespoon freshly grated orange zest
1 silver or gold coin
Sesame seed, as needed
Whole blanched almonds, as needed

In a small bowl sprinkle yeast over the warm water and let stand to soften (about 5 minutes). Fill a sifter with 5 cups flour and sift into a large mixing bowl; make a well in center of flour. In a separate bowl combine yeast mixture, milk, the 1 cup butter, beaten whole eggs, sugar, salt, nutmeg, cinnamon, and orange zest; mix ingredients until well blended.

Slowly pour egg mixture into flour well, mixing ingredients together with hands until thoroughly blended. Turn onto a lightly floured board and knead until smooth and firm, adding more flour as needed to achieve correct texture. Butter a large bowl. Form dough into a ball and place in greased bowl; lightly brush top of dough with butter, cover bowl with a tea towel, and set in warm place to rise until doubled in bulk (about 2 hours).

Punch down dough, turn onto a lightly floured board, and knead gently. Butter a baking sheet. Shape dough into a large round loaf, burying the coin in the center. Place on baking sheet. Cover with tea towel and set in a warm place to rise until almost doubled in bulk (1 hour).

Preheat oven to 350° F. Brush loaf with egg yolk and sprinkle generously with sesame seed. Arrange almonds on top to form the number of the upcoming year. Bake until a knife inserted in center comes out clean and top is golden brown (about 1 hour). Slide onto wire rack to cool.

Makes 1 large loaf

Poseidon, The God of the Sea

The awesome figure of Poseidon
stands unchallenged
as God of the Sea.
Mercy and wrath are his
to dispense as he deems.
His bronze statue stands in Athens,
astride,
with arms magnificently poised,
apparently having flung his trident.
Little wonder Homer titled him
Earth-Shaker.
Ensconced in the land of the gods,
Poseidon, we worship him,
for his domain of the sea, and
its bounty we receive.

POSEIDON AND THE FOODS FROM THE SEA

The coastline of Greece stretches some 2500 miles. For centuries many Greeks have depended upon the wealth of the sea for their livelihoods and for stocking their larders. Greek cooks have taken that precious bounty and created such memorable dishes as psari plaki, *the baked fish with tomato that is traditionally served on Palm Sunday, and* garides me feta, *succulent pink prawns topped with feta cheese.*

Some of the fish most prized in the Greek islands are not available fresh in the markets of North America. We must do without the delicious red mullet (barbouni), *the smooth-fleshed bass* (synargida), *and the unforgettable* petalia, *which is sun-dried in my father's native Mesolongion—a picturesque port on the Gulf of Corinth formerly known as* Missalonghi—*and eaten in the winter months when the rough seas hinder fishing.*

Fortunately, many fish found in North American markets— halibut, striped bass, sea bass—may be successfully substituted for the Greek varieties. Eels, octopus, salt cod, and squid, all of which are popular throughout Greece, also are available here. So, happily, Greek-American fish cookery does not suffer for lack of a Mediterranean catch.

It does sometimes suffer from misunderstanding, however. There are those who believe that Greeks do nothing more than drench fish in olive oil and lemon juice. They are unaware of the great seafood recipes that have been part of Greek culture for centuries. Athenaeus, for example, wrote of "electric ray stewed in oil, wine, and fragrant herbs, with a little grated cheese." Who can dispute such a triumph of taste?

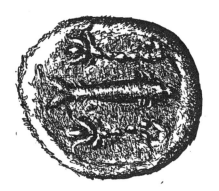

Fish and Shrimp

The most important consideration when preparing fish is that the fish itself be impeccably fresh. A number of different kinds of fish appear in the following recipes—halibut, striped bass, sea bass, trout. In general, however, these dishes can be adapted to your favorite fish and to what is best in the market. Shrimp are seldom sold fresh, so rely on a good fishmonger to direct you to the finest quality.

Baked Fish, Kalamata Style
Psari Fournou à la Kalamai

The city of Kalamata, called *Kalamai* in Greek, is on the southwest coast of the Peloponnesus. It has balmy weather year-round, palm trees, an old tile-clad train station, and a harbor lined with tavernas. You are certain to find this dish there.

1 cup raisins
1 cup white wine
4 halibut fillets (about 6 oz each)
Salt and freshly ground pepper, to taste
Juice of 1 lemon
3 large onions, thinly sliced
½ cup water
1 can (16 oz) plum tomatoes, chopped,
*   with their liquid*
½ cup olive oil
4 whole cloves
4 slices lemon

In a small bowl combine raisins and wine; set aside. Place fillets on a plate and sprinkle on both sides with salt, pepper, and lemon juice.

Preheat oven to 350° F. In a skillet combine onions and the water. Bring to a gentle boil, cover, reduce heat to low, and simmer until soft (about 10 minutes). Add tomatoes, oil, cloves, and raisins and wine; cook, uncovered, over low heat until flavors are blended (about 15 minutes).

Select a baking dish in which fillets will fit side by side. Spoon enough tomato-onion mixture into bottom of dish to form a thin layer. Arrange fillets on top and cover with remaining tomato-onion mixture. Place 1 lemon slice on each fillet.

Bake until fish flakes easily with a fork and sauce is bubbly (30 to 45 minutes). Serve hot.

Serves 4

Fish Soup

Psarosoupa

My earliest recollection of fish soup is from when I was a small child in Chicago. On Halsted Street, in the center of Greektown, there was a wonderful fish market. The counters seemed to be endless, and—I swear—all the fish in the world's oceans were in that shop. As my mother, Anna, and I returned with our newspaper-wrapped bounty, the neighbors would always exclaim, "Ah, Anna's cooking fish soup again." Here is my mother's recipe. Prepare the Garlic Sauce several hours in advance so that it will be well chilled. Note that this recipe yields both a first and second course—broth for first course and poached fish and vegetables for the entrée.

1 cup olive oil
2 large onions, thickly sliced
2 stalks celery, chopped
4 cloves garlic, crushed
6 tomatoes, peeled, seeded, and chopped
2 bay leaves
1 sprig thyme or 1 teaspoon dried thyme, crushed
4 sprigs fresh parsley
2 cups bottled clam juice
1 cup dry white wine
6 cups water, or as needed
3 or 4 fish heads, preferably cod or sea bass
8 medium potatoes, peeled
12 leeks (white part only)
Salt, to taste
5 or 6 lemons
2 pounds eel, skinned and cut in 2-inch-thick slices
2 pounds fresh cod fillets (about 1 inch thick)
1 whole striped bass or sea bass (about 2 lb), cleaned
Flour, for coating fish
Garlic Sauce (see page 176)

Select a large, heavy-bottomed stockpot that is large enough to hold a whole bass. Pour in oil and heat over medium-high heat. Add onions, celery, and garlic; cook, stirring, until onions are translucent (about 5 minutes). Add tomatoes, bay leaves, thyme, parsley, clam juice, wine, the water, and fish heads. Bring to a boil, reduce heat, and simmer, uncovered, 25 minutes.

Add potatoes and leeks to pot and simmer until leeks are tender (about 15 minutes). Remove leeks to a plate. Continue to simmer potatoes until they are tender (about 15 minutes); remove potatoes to plate with leeks.

Strain broth and return to pot. Add salt, juice of 1 lemon, eel slices, and cod. Add more water if needed to cover fish and bring to a rapid boil. Lower heat slightly and simmer until eel easily flakes with a fork (15 to 20 minutes). Remove with a slotted utensil and keep warm. Cook cod about 10 minutes longer, then remove from broth.

While eel and cod are cooking, sprinkle bass with juice of 1 lemon, season with salt, and dust

Continued–

with flour to coat lightly. Wrap bass in a double thickness of cheesecloth and tie ends securely. Once eel and cod have been removed from broth, carefully lower cheesecloth-wrapped bass into it. Simmer until cooked (20 to 40 minutes, depending upon thickness of fish).

Lift bass from broth and lay it on a flat surface. Unwrap cheesecloth and transfer bass to a heated platter. Dip reserved eel and cod in broth to reheat, then arrange on platter with bass. Reheat leeks in the same manner and place on a separate heated plate. Keep fish and leeks warm. Heat broth to serving temperature; then drop cooked potatoes into it to reheat. Ladle broth into individual soup bowls and put a potato in each bowl. Serve broth as a first course. For second course, cut remaining lemons in half and ring edge of fish platter with them. Arrange leeks and Garlic Sauce alongside.

Serves 8 as first course and entrée

Stuffed Striped Bass

Psari Yemisto

In Greece striped bass is a favorite fish for stuffing, but sea bass works well too. Sautéed greens and a dessert of fresh fruit complement this exquisite dish. Chill a bottle of dry white wine to serve with the meal.

Currant-Rice Stuffing (see following recipe)
1 whole striped bass (about 4 lb),
    cleaned
Salt and freshly ground pepper, to taste
Melted butter, as needed
Juice of 1 lemon
1 cup white wine
½ cup olive oil
1 tablespoon minced fresh oregano
2 tablespoons chopped fresh parsley
Lemon slices and Kalamata olives, for
    garnish

Prepare stuffing and let cool. Preheat oven to 375° F.

Sprinkle fish cavity with salt and pepper, then fill with stuffing. Skewer or sew cavity closed. Brush a small casserole with butter and put remaining stuffing in it. Drizzle stuffing with butter, cover with foil, and set aside.

Brush butter on a baking pan large enough to hold fish flat. Place stuffed fish in pan and brush lightly with butter. Sprinkle with salt, pepper, and lemon juice. In a small bowl combine wine, oil, oregano, and parsley; whisk to blend, then pour over and around fish.

Place fish and casserole in oven. Bake fish, basting frequently with pan juices, until it flakes easily with a fork (50 minutes to 1 hour, depending upon thickness of fish). Transfer to a heated platter and garnish with lemon slices and olives.

Serves 6 to 8

Currant-Rice Stuffing

1 cup dried currants
¼ cup brandy
About 4½ cups bottled clam juice
2 cups long-grain white rice
Butter, for sautéing
1 cup chopped onion
3 tablespoons chopped fresh parsley
1 cup minced celery
½ cup pine nuts
Salt and freshly ground pepper, to taste

In a small bowl combine currants and brandy and set aside. In a medium saucepan over high heat, bring 4 cups of the clam juice to a boil. Add rice and stir well. Cover, reduce heat to low, and cook until rice is tender and liquid is absorbed (about 20 minutes).

When rice is cooked, place a large skillet over medium heat. Melt butter in skillet and add onion, parsley, and celery. Sauté until vegetables are golden (about 7 minutes). Add cooked rice, currants and brandy, and pine nuts; mix well and season with salt and pepper. Add additional clam juice as needed to moisten stuffing. Cool before stuffing fish.

Fish Baked with Tomatoes
Psari Plaki

GGGGGGGGGGGGGGGGGGGGGGGGGGGGGGG

*T*he Greek Orthodox calendar is marked with scores of holy days, but none are more important than those leading up to Easter. Greek families traditionally sit down to a platter of *psari plaki* for Palm Sunday dinner.

*½ cup olive oil, plus olive oil for baking
    dish
1 cup finely chopped fresh parsley
3 pounds halibut or sea bass fillets (6 to
    8 fillets)
Salt and freshly ground pepper, to taste
Juice of 1 lemon
4 medium-sized ripe tomatoes, peeled
3 onions, thinly sliced
2 cloves garlic, minced
1 cup dry white wine
1 cup bottled clam juice
Minced fresh oregano, to taste*

Preheat oven to 350° F. Select a baking dish in which fillets will fit side by side. Oil dish and strew ½ cup of the parsley evenly over the bottom. Place fillets in dish and sprinkle with salt, pepper, and lemon juice.

Chop 2 of the tomatoes; in a medium bowl combine chopped tomatoes, onions, garlic, the remaining parsley, wine, clam juice, and the ½ cup oil. Mix well and pour over fish. Slice remaining 2 tomatoes and arrange over fillets. Sprinkle with oregano.

Bake until fish flakes easily with a fork (30 to 45 minutes).

Serves 6 to 8

Baked Pompano
Psari Psito

GGGGGGGGGGGGGGGGGGGGGGGGGGGGGGGGGG

*M*y father loved both to cook and to eat fish. This delicious recipe for pompano is one of his finest creations. From May to October Greek immigrants in Tarpon Springs, Florida, pull silvery flat-sided pompanos from Gulf Coast waters. If you can't find pompanos, substitute a whole 4- to 5-pound snapper and increase the baking time to 45 minutes to 1 hour.

*1 cup olive oil, plus olive oil for baking
    dish
4 small (1 to 1½ lb each) pompanos,
    cleaned
Salt and freshly ground pepper, to taste
Juice of 2 lemons
6 green onions, finely chopped
2 tablespoons minced fresh parsley
3 cloves garlic, minced
1 tablespoon minced fresh oregano
½ cup each bottled clam juice and dry
    white wine*

Preheat oven to 375° F. Oil a baking dish large enough to hold fish side by side. Place pompanos in pan and sprinkle with salt, pepper, and lemon juice. In a small bowl combine onions, parsley, garlic, oregano, and the 1 cup oil; mix well and pour over the fish, distributing evenly. Combine clam juice and wine and spoon over fish.

Bake, basting often, until fish flakes easily with a fork (about 30 minutes).

Serves 4

Sole with Raisin Sauce
Psari me Saltsa Stafedes

GGGGGGGGGGGGGGGGGGGGGGGGGGGGGGGGGG

*S*erve these spinach-filled rolls with pilaf (see page 67) and a green salad.

> *White Sauce With Raisins (see page 175)*
> *3 pounds spinach*
> *Butter, for sautéing and for baking dish*
> *6 green onions, finely chopped*
> *1 clove garlic, minced*
> *3 tablespoons chopped fresh parsley*
> *1 teaspoon dried fines herbes, crushed*
> *8 sole fillets (about 4 oz each)*
> *Salt and freshly ground pepper, to taste*

Prepare sauce and set aside. Preheat oven to 350° F.

Trim stems from spinach leaves and wash leaves well. Place leaves, dripping wet, in a large pot. Cover tightly and cook over medium-low heat until wilted. Drain, press out excess moisture, and chop.

In a large skillet over medium heat, melt butter. Add spinach, onions, garlic, and parsley; sauté until onion is translucent (about 5 minutes). Add fines herbes and cook 5 minutes longer; remove from heat.

Sprinkle fillets with salt and pepper. Place about ½ cup of the spinach mixture in center of each fillet, roll up, and secure roll with a toothpick. Butter 4 individual ramekins (or 1 large baking dish) and arrange 2 fish rolls in each. Spoon sauce over rolls. Bake until fish flakes easily with a fork (20 to 30 minutes).

Serves 4

Trout in Foil
Psari sto Harti

GGGGGGGGGGGGGGGGGGGGGGGGGGGGGGGGGGGGG

A mushroom-onion stuffing infuses these foil-wrapped trout with an intense flavor. Let guests unwrap the packets at the table.

> *3 tablespoons butter*
> *4 green onions (including some green top), finely chopped*
> *1 stalk celery, finely chopped*
> *1 teaspoon chopped fresh parsley*
> *6 medium-sized fresh mushrooms, finely chopped*
> *Salt and freshly ground pepper, to taste*
> *Minced fresh oregano, to taste*
> *⅓ cup dry white wine*
> *4 medium trout, cleaned*
> *2 lemons, halved*
> *Olive oil, to taste*

Preheat oven to 400° F. In a skillet over medium-high heat, melt butter. Add onions, celery, parsley, and mushrooms; sauté until vegetables are glazed (about 5 minutes). Season with salt, pepper, and oregano. Add wine, reduce heat to low, and simmer 10 minutes. Remove from heat and cool.

Stuff each trout with one fourth of mushroom mixture. Secure trout closed with skewers. For each trout ready a double-thick sheet of aluminum foil large enough to enclose fish. Place trout in center; sprinkle with salt, pepper, and oregano and squeeze juice of ½ lemon over top. Drizzle with oil. Fold aluminum foil around trout to secure tightly. Place in baking pan and bake 15 minutes.

Serves 4

Fresh Cod with Spinach and Garlic Sauce

Bakaliaros me Spanaki

Greeks include fresh greens in their meals as often as possible. Here spinach forms a bed for cod steaks. Prepare the Garlic Sauce several hours in advance so that the flavors have time to blend and the sauce is well chilled. Offer a tossed green salad and crusty bread as accompaniments.

1 cup Garlic Sauce (see page 176)
6 tablespoons olive oil, plus olive oil for
    baking dish
2 pounds spinach, trimmed and finely
    chopped
6 to 8 green onions, chopped
1 clove garlic, minced
Pinch dried oregano, crushed
6 cod steaks (each about 3/4 in. thick)
Juice of 1 lemon

Prepare Garlic Sauce and chill. Preheat oven to 350° F.

In a large skillet over medium heat, warm 3 tablespoons of the oil. Add spinach, onions, garlic, and oregano; sauté until spinach is tender (about 10 minutes). Remove from heat.

Oil a baking dish in which cod steaks will fit side by side. Spread spinach mixture evenly on bottom. Arrange steaks on top. Drizzle lemon juice and the remaining oil over steaks. Bake until fish flakes easily with a fork (35 to 45 minutes).

Serve each steak on a bed of spinach. Top with Garlic Sauce. Pass remaining sauce.

Serves 6

Fresh Cod Baked with Currants

Bakaliaros Plaki

Currants are not native to Greece but have become a favorite ingredient. Serve cod with plenty of crusty bread for dunking in the delicious sauce.

1/2 cup dried currants
1 cup dry white wine
1/2 cup olive oil, plus olive oil for baking dish
6 cod steaks (each about 3/4 in. thick)
Salt and freshly ground pepper, to taste
2 cloves garlic, crushed
Juice of 1 lemon
2 onions, thinly sliced
3 tablespoons chopped fresh parsley
1 can (16 oz) plum tomatoes, chopped,
    with their liquid
2 whole cloves

Preheat oven to 400° F. In a small bowl combine currants and wine; set aside. Oil a baking dish in which cod steaks will fit side by side.

Place fish steaks in baking dish. Season with salt and pepper, then rub with garlic and drizzle with lemon juice.

In a large skillet over medium-high heat, warm the 1/2 cup oil. Add onions, parsley, and tomatoes; cook until onions are soft (5 to 6 minutes). Add cloves and currants and wine; simmer over medium heat 5 minutes. Pour sauce over fish steaks.

Bake until fish flakes easily with a fork (35 to 45 minutes), basting several times during cooking. Transfer fish to serving plates and spoon sauce over top.

Serves 6

Halibut with Shrimp Sauce
Psari me Saltsa Garides

*I*n Greek villages fish markets are where people meet to exchange news of family and friends and to select the very best of the local catch. In summer when the fishermen go to sea every day, the choices are many and the competition for customers is heated. For this delicately flavored dish, you will need to search your own local fish markets for fresh halibut or other favorite white-fish steaks.

*1 cup Basic White Sauce for Fish
    (see page 174)
4 halibut steaks (about 6 oz each)
Salt and freshly ground pepper
Flour, for dredging
5 tablespoons butter
Juice of 1 lemon
6 green onions (including some green
    top), finely chopped
2 stalks celery, finely chopped
2 tablespoons finely chopped parsley
1 clove garlic, minced
¼ pound small shrimp, peeled
1 large ripe tomato, peeled and chopped
½ cup dry white wine or sherry
1 tablespoon minced fresh oregano or
    1 teaspoon dried oregano, crushed*

Prepare white sauce and set aside. Preheat oven to 375° F.

Sprinkle fish with salt and pepper, then dredge lightly in flour. In a large skillet over medium heat, melt 2 tablespoons of the butter. Gently brown fish steaks on both sides. Remove to a platter and drizzle with lemon juice.

In a second skillet over medium heat, melt the remaining butter. Add onions, celery, parsley, and garlic; sauté until onions are translucent (about 5 minutes). Add shrimp, tomato, reserved white sauce, wine, and oregano. Stir well and simmer 10 minutes. Season with salt and pepper.

Arrange fish steaks side by side in a baking dish. Spoon sauce over steaks. Bake until fish flakes easily with a fork (20 to 25 minutes).

Serves 4

Shrimp with Feta in Casserole

Garides me Feta

GGGGGGGGGGGGGGGGGGGGGGGGGGGGGGGGGGGGGGGGGGGGGGGGGGGGGGGGGGGGGGGGGGGGGGGGG

This casserole of feta-topped baked shrimp is served throughout the Greek islands, where shrimp have been caught in nets since ancient times. For this very special dish you will need vine-ripened tomatoes, fresh oregano, and the best-quality shrimp you can find.

2 pounds medium shrimp, peeled and
    deveined
Juice of 1 lemon
1 cup olive oil
1 large clove garlic, minced
2 bunches (about 12) green onions,
    finely chopped
1 stalk celery, finely chopped
2 tablespoons finely chopped fresh
    parsley
3 medium-sized ripe tomatoes, peeled
    and chopped, plus 1 large ripe
    tomato, peeled and cored
1 cup bottled clam juice
Salt and freshly ground pepper, to taste
Butter, for sautéing
1 tablespoon minced fresh oregano
½ cup dry white wine
1 pound feta cheese, crumbled

Preheat oven to 400° F. Place shrimp in a bowl and pour lemon juice over top; set aside.

In a skillet over medium-high heat, warm oil. Add garlic, onions, celery, parsley, and chopped tomatoes; cook until onions are soft (4 or 5 minutes). Reduce heat and simmer, uncovered, 20 minutes. Add clam juice and simmer 5 minutes longer. Season with salt and pepper; remove from heat.

In a second skillet over medium-high heat, melt butter. Add shrimp and sauté just until they turn pink (about 1 minute). Remove from heat.

Pour tomato mixture into a casserole. Place whole tomato in center of dish and surround evenly with sautéed shrimp. Sprinkle oregano over entire casserole, then drizzle wine over and around shrimp. Sprinkle feta over shrimp and tomato centerpiece. Bake until cheese melts (about 15 minutes).

To serve, carefully lift out shrimp with spatula so that melted feta stays intact and place on individual serving plates. Spoon some sauce from casserole alongside.

Serves 6

Shrimp Pilaf
Garides Pilafi

This pilaf simmers in a sauce of tomatoes and full-bodied sherry. The Greeks who live on Cyprus, an island-country near Turkey, bottle a number of high-quality sherries that are suitable for drinking or cooking. Look for Greek Cypriot sherry in a well-stocked wine shop.

2 pounds medium shrimp
Juice of 1 lemon
1 cup water
½ cup butter
6 green onions, chopped
2 stalks celery, chopped
1 clove garlic, minced
2 tablespoons chopped fresh parsley
1 tablespoon minced fresh oregano or
    1 teaspoon dried oregano, crushed
Salt and freshly ground pepper, to taste
4 ripe tomatoes, peeled and chopped
1 tablespoon tomato paste
1 cup dry sherry
Rice Pilaf (see page 67), made with
    4 cups bottled clam juice

Peel and devein shrimp, reserving shells. Place shrimp in a bowl and pour lemon juice over top. Place shells in a saucepan with the water and bring to a boil over high heat; boil a few minutes, then strain and reserve liquid.

In a large skillet over medium heat, melt ¼ cup of the butter. Add onions, celery, garlic, and parsley; sauté until onions are translucent (about 5 minutes). Add shrimp, oregano, salt, and pepper; sauté 3 or 4 minutes. Stir in tomatoes, tomato paste, the remaining butter, sherry, and reserved shrimp-shell broth. Cover and simmer until flavors are well blended (about 25 minutes).

Meanwhile, prepare pilaf, using clam juice for the liquid.

For each serving, pack hot rice into individual molds, cool slightly, then unmold on a serving plate. Spoon shrimp sauce over rice molds.

Serves 6

Shrimp on Skewers
Garides Souvlakia

The town of Khania (also known as *Canea*) on the northwestern coast of Crete boasts narrow streets, fourteenth-century Venetian homes, and massive stone walls protecting the harbor. In the many tavernas, the townspeople can often be found sitting down to a plate of these garlicky shrimp, vine-ripened tomatoes topped with feta, and glasses of chilled white retsina.

24 large shrimp, peeled and deveined
3 cloves garlic, minced
3 tablespoons chopped fresh parsley
2 tablespoons chopped fresh oregano
½ cup olive oil
¼ cup brandy or dry white wine
Salt and freshly ground pepper, to taste
Lemon wedges, for accompaniment

In a large bowl combine all ingredients except lemon wedges. Mix well and marinate at least 1 hour, or cover and refrigerate up to 4 hours.

Preheat broiler. Remove shrimp, reserving marinade; thread 6 shrimp onto each of 4 metal skewers. Place on a broiler rack with a pan underneath to catch drippings. Pour marinade over shrimp. Broil about 3 inches from heat, basting with marinade and turning once, until golden on both sides (about 10 minutes total cooking time).

Slide shrimp off skewers onto individual serving plates. Pour pan juices over and serve immediately with lemon wedges.

Serves 4

Lobster Variation Substitute 2 pounds lobster meat, cut in chunks, for shrimp.

Seafood Omelet

Avga me Psariou

For a sumptuous luncheon or midnight supper, lightly bind cooked scallops, shrimp, lobster chunks, and/or crabmeat with cream and fold into an omelet. If desired, garnish plate with broiled tomato halves.

> *5 tablespoons butter*
> *2 green onions, finely chopped*
> *1 tablespoon minced fresh parsley*
> *1 tablespoon flour*
> *3 tablespoons half-and-half*
> *Dash dried oregano, crushed*
> *1 cup freshly cooked mixed shellfish*
> *   of choice*
> *6 eggs, beaten*

In a small skillet over medium heat, melt 2 tablespoons of the butter. Add onions and parsley and sauté until onions are translucent (about 5 minutes). Dissolve flour in 2 tablespoons of the half-and-half and add to skillet with oregano. Cook over low heat, stirring, until thickened (2 to 3 minutes). Add shellfish and cook just until heated through and all liquid has evaporated. Remove from heat.

In a large omelet pan or skillet over medium heat, melt the remaining butter. Whisk the remaining half-and-half into eggs and pour into pan; tilt pan to distribute eggs evenly and shake pan gently to keep them from sticking. Reduce heat slightly; lift edges of omelet with a spatula to allow uncooked egg to flow underneath. When eggs are almost cooked but still creamy on top, place shellfish mixture in a line down center. Fold omelet sides over filling and cook 1 or 2 minutes longer.

Carefully slide omelet onto a heated platter and serve.

Serves 2 or 3 as a light entrée

Salt Cod, Octopus, Squid, and Eel

*T*hese denizens of the sea are well-loved by the Greeks and their Mediterranean neighbors. If you have never prepared them before, give them a chance now. You will wonder why you didn't discover these marvelous seafoods sooner.

Squid is widely available, but salt cod, octopus, and eel may be more difficult to locate. Check well-stocked fish markets, especially those in southern European immigrant neighborhoods. Eel and octopus can also be found in many Asian fish markets.

Salt Cod Patties with Garlic Sauce
Bakaliaros Kefte Skordalia

*T*he salt cod I prefer comes packed in a small wooden box, but any good-quality, boneless salt cod will do. For an hors d'oeuvre, form the potato-cod mixture into small balls the size of walnuts and fry as directed for the patties. Note that the salt cod needs to soak overnight.

> 1 pound boneless salt cod
> Garlic Sauce (see page 176)
> 1 bay leaf
> 1 yellow onion, quartered
> 2 cups mashed cooked potatoes
> 2 green onions, finely chopped
> 2 tablespoons finely chopped fresh
>   parsley
> 1 egg
> Flour, for coating
> 3 tablespoons butter
> 2 tablespoons olive oil

Cover cod with cold water and soak over-night in refrigerator, changing water once or twice. Prepare Garlic Sauce, cover, and chill well.

Drain cod and place in a saucepan. Add water to cover, bring to a boil, and drain. Return cod to saucepan, add bay leaf and yellow onion, and bring to a boil. Reduce heat and simmer 20 minutes. Drain in a colander, discarding onion and bay leaf. When cool enough to handle, mash and squeeze cod with your fingers until all water is removed and fish is completely broken up.

In a large bowl combine cod, potato, green onions, parsley, and egg. Knead thoroughly. Turn onto a floured board and form into 8 patties. Dust patties with flour.

In a large skillet over medium heat, melt butter with oil. Fry patties, turning once, until golden brown on both sides (about 10 minutes total cooking time). Serve on a platter with Garlic Sauce in a bowl alongside.

Serves 4

Salt Cod in Casserole with White Sauce
Bakaliaros me Aspri Saltsa

Greek cooks often prepare salt-cod dishes in the wintertime, when the seas are too rough for fishing. The best salt cod comes packed in a small wooden box, but any good-quality, boneless salt cod will do for this hearty casserole. Note that the salt cod needs to soak overnight.

2 pounds boneless salt cod
4 large potatoes
1 bay leaf
1 onion, quartered
Basic White Sauce for Fish (see page 174)
2 cloves garlic, crushed
Olive oil, for baking dish
Salt and freshly ground pepper to taste
Butter, as needed
1 teaspoon dried oregano, crushed
3 tablespoons minced fresh parsley
½ cup dry white wine
½ cup freshly grated kefalotyri or
    Parmesan cheese

Cover cod with cold water and soak overnight in refrigerator, changing water once or twice.

Boil potatoes in water to cover until just beginning to soften (about 20 minutes). Drain, cool, peel, and slice; set aside.

Preheat oven to 300° F. Drain cod and place in a saucepan. Add water to cover, bring to a boil, and drain again. Return cod to saucepan, add bay leaf and onion, and bring to a boil. Reduce heat and simmer 20 minutes.

While cod is simmering, prepare white sauce, adding the crushed garlic when seasoning with salt and pepper; set aside.

Drain cod in a colander, discarding onion and bay leaf. When cool enough to handle, flake fish with fingers.

Oil a 9- by 13-inch baking dish. Layer half of the flaked cod in bottom of dish. Layer potato slices on top; sprinkle with salt and pepper. Dot generously with butter. Top with remaining cod and sprinkle with oregano and parsley. Drizzle wine evenly over surface, then pour white sauce over the top. Sprinkle with cheese.

Bake until top is lightly browned and sauce is bubbly (about 1 hour).

Serves 8

Baked Salt Cod with Tomato Sauce

Bakaliaros tou Fournou

╔═══╗

*T*hese cod patties can also be panfried, with the tomato sauce served in a bowl alongside. Round out the meal with crusty bread and a salad of curly endive. Try to find the salt cod that comes packed in small wooden boxes. If you can't find it, any good, boneless salt cod will do. Note that the salt cod needs to soak overnight.

1 pound boneless salt cod
1 bay leaf
1 yellow onion, quartered
Tomato Sauce (see following recipe)
3 cloves garlic, minced
6 green onions, finely chopped
3 tablespoons minced fresh parsley
1 egg, lightly beaten
1 cup fine dried bread crumbs
Salt and freshly ground pepper, to taste
Flour, for dusting
2 tablespoons butter
2 tablespoons olive oil, plus oil for baking dish

Cover cod with cold water and soak overnight in the refrigerator, changing water once or twice.

Preheat oven to 425° F. Drain cod and place in a saucepan. Add water to cover, bring to a boil, and drain. Return cod to saucepan, add bay leaf and yellow onion, and bring to a boil. Reduce heat and simmer 20 minutes.

While cod is simmering prepare Tomato Sauce.

Drain cod in a colander, discarding onion and bay leaf. When cool enough to handle, flake fish with fingers.

In a mixing bowl combine flaked cod, garlic, green onions, parsley, egg, and bread crumbs. Season with salt and pepper and mix well. Form mixture into 4 patties and dust lightly with flour.

In a large skillet over medium-high heat, melt butter with the 2 tablespoons oil. Fry patties until lightly browned on both sides, turning once.

Oil a baking dish or casserole in which patties will fit side by side. Arrange patties in dish and pour Tomato Sauce over the top.

Bake until heated through and bubbly (about 30 minutes).

Serves 4

Tomato Sauce

¹⁄₄ cup olive oil
1 onion, thinly sliced
3 tablespoons minced fresh parsley
1 teaspoon dried fines herbes, crushed
1 can (16 oz) plum tomatoes, chopped, with their liquid
¹⁄₂ cup dry white wine
Salt and freshly ground pepper, to taste

In a skillet over medium-high heat, warm oil. Add onion and sauté until translucent (about 5 minutes). Add remaining ingredients, reduce heat, and simmer 20 minutes.

Octopus Pilaf
Oktapodi Pilafi

*F*ish markets in North America almost always sell octopus cleaned, with the beak, viscera, and ink sac removed. Some shops also sell it prepounded, in which case you can omit the tenderizing step.

> 2 pounds dressed octopus
> ½ cup plus 2 tablespoons butter
> 2 medium onions, minced
> 1 clove garlic, minced
> 1 bay leaf
> Pinch dried oregano, crushed
> ½ teaspoon dried fines herbes, crushed
> 2 tablespoons tomato paste
> 1 can (16 oz) plum tomatoes with their
>   liquid
> 1 cup dry white wine
> Salt and freshly ground pepper, to taste
> 3½ cups water
> 2 cups long-grain white rice

Remove and discard skin from octopus. With a meat mallet or other heavy instrument, pound octopus until flesh feels somewhat soft to the touch. Cut in 1-inch cubes and set aside.

In a large saucepan over medium heat, melt the ½ cup butter. Add onions and sauté until golden brown (about 7 minutes). Add garlic, bay leaf, oregano, fines herbes, and octopus. Sauté 3 or 4 minutes; stir in tomato paste, whole tomatoes with juice, wine, salt, and pepper. Stir well, cover, and simmer over low heat until octopus is tender (about 1 hour).

Remove ½ cup of liquid from saucepan holding octopus and place in a second saucepan with the water and the 2 tablespoons butter. Bring to a boil and add rice. Stir well, cover, and reduce heat to low. Cook until rice is tender and liquid is absorbed (about 20 minutes).

Pack hot rice into individual molds, cool slightly, then unmold on serving plates. Spoon octopus with sauce over top.

Serves 4 to 6

Octopus in Wine
Oktapodi Krassato

᠎🏵️

Select a full-bodied red wine for cooking the octopus. The octopus cubes can be served hot with pilaf (see page 67) as an entrée, or chilled and offered as an hors d'oeuvre with lemon wedges. North American fish markets sell octopus cleaned (beak, viscera, and ink sac removed) and sometimes prepounded. If you buy prepounded octopus, omit the tenderizing step.

2 pounds dressed octopus
¼ cup olive oil
2 medium onions, finely chopped
2 cloves garlic, minced
2 tablespoons chopped fresh parsley
2 bay leaves
½ teaspoon dried oregano, crushed
Pinch dried thyme, crushed
1 cup red wine
1½ tablespoons freshly squeezed lemon
   juice
Salt and freshly ground pepper, to taste

Remove and discard skin from octopus. With a meat mallet or other heavy instrument, pound octopus until flesh feels somewhat soft to the touch. Cut in 1-inch cubes and set aside.

In a saucepan over medium-high heat, warm oil. Add onions, garlic, parsley, bay leaves, oregano, and thyme; sauté until golden brown (8 to 10 minutes). Add octopus and wine and cook over medium heat 10 minutes.

Add lemon juice and just enough water to cover octopus. Bring to a boil, cover, reduce heat, and simmer until octopus is tender (about 1 hour).

Season with salt and pepper. Serve hot or chilled.

Serves 4 as an entrée or 8 as an hors d'oeuvre

Stuffed Squid
Kalamaria Yemista

GGGGGGGGGGGGGGGGGGGGGGGGGGGGGGGGGGGG

*T*his unusual dish is very simple to prepare, since the squid are stuffed only with their own tentacles. Accompany the squid with Pilaf (see page 67) and Boiled Greens with Lemon Juice and Olive Oil (see page 61).

3 pounds squid
Flour, for dusting
½ cup olive oil
1 cup red wine vinegar

Rinse squid under cold water. Gently pull on head portion and the entrails will slide free from body. Place head portion on a cutting board and cut off tentacles just above the eyes. Remove and discard hard beak from base of tentacles; set tentacles aside. Discard head and entrails. Pull transparent quill from body and discard. Rinse squid inside and out. Peel off mottled skin from body and fins.

Dry squid and tentacles well, then stuff a set of tentacles into each squid body. Dust squid with flour, shaking off excess.

In a large skillet over high heat, warm oil. Add squid and sauté on all sides until they turn a pale pink. Pour in vinegar, cover, and reduce heat to low. Simmer until sauce is thick and squid is very tender (about 45 minutes).

Serves 6

Broiled Eel
Cheli tis Skaras

GGGGGGGGGGGGGGGGGGGGGGGGGGGGGGGGGGGG

*M*ention eel to a Greek and he or she is overcome by nostalgia. Eel is holiday fare, the centerpiece of the traditional Christmas Eve meal in many parts of the islands. The flesh is luxuriously rich and sweet, the texture is firm, the color is snowy white. Serve this classic preparation with a salad of tomatoes and feta cheese and a bowl of Lima Bean Plaki (see page 58).

2 to 2½ pounds eel
Salt and freshly ground pepper, to taste
Olive oil, as needed
Freshly squeezed lemon juice, to taste
Minced fresh parsley and lemon wedges,
*   for garnish*

Preheat broiler. Skin eel and cut in 2-inch-thick slices. Sprinkle slices with salt and pepper and brush with oil.

Broil eel on both sides, turning once, until flesh flakes easily with a fork (10 to 15 minutes total cooking time).

Place on a heated platter and sprinkle to taste with lemon juice, salt, and pepper. Garnish with parsley and lemon wedges and serve at once.

Serves 4

Eel in Tomato Sauce

Cheli me Domates

🔲🔲

*T*he ancient Greeks, who could find neither roe nor milt in the eel, anointed Zeus the father of these seemingly parentless marine residents. Here the Sky God's offspring is cooked in a full-flavored tomato sauce. Artichokes and Rice (see page 57), crusty bread, feta cheese slices, and Kalamata olives are all you need to complete the feast.

½ cup olive oil
2 medium onions, minced
2 cloves garlic, minced
2 tablespoons minced fresh parsley
6 ripe tomatoes, peeled and chopped
2 bay leaves
Pinch dried thyme, crushed
Pinch ground cloves
½ cup bottled clam juice
Salt and freshly ground pepper, to taste
3 pounds eel
Flour, for dusting
Butter, for sautéing
1 cup dry white wine
Dash brandy

In a large skillet over medium-high heat, warm oil. Add onions, garlic, and parsley; sauté until onions are golden (about 8 minutes). Add tomatoes, bay leaves, thyme, and cloves; stir to mix well. Pour in clam juice and season with salt and pepper. Simmer 10 minutes.

Meanwhile, skin eel and cut in 2-inch-thick slices. Dry with paper towels, then lightly dust with flour. In a skillet over medium heat, melt butter. Add eel and sauté on both sides until golden (about 5 minutes total cooking time).

Add eel slices and wine to tomato mixture, stirring gently to coat slices completely. Bring to a simmer, cover, and cook over low heat 30 minutes. Remove from heat, add brandy, cover, and let stand a few minutes.

To serve, lift eel slices out of sauce with a slotted spoon and arrange on a heated platter. Spoon hot sauce over slices.

Serves 4 to 6

Eel

Tighanito

I find that a dollop of garlic sauce is an excellent counterpoint to the richness of eel, although this dish is also delicious served plain. Uncork a bottle of your best white retsina to drink with the meal.

½ recipe Garlic Sauce Evoula
    (see page 177), optional
3 pounds eel
Juice of 2 lemons
¼ cup dry white wine
Salt and freshly ground pepper, to taste
Flour, for dusting
Butter, for sautéing
Minced fresh parsley, Kalamata olives,
    and lemon wedges, for garnish

Prepare garlic sauce (if used), cover, and chill well.

Skin eel and cut in 2-inch-thick slices. Place in a bowl and add lemon juice and wine. Turn eel in marinade to coat evenly and let stand 1 hour.

Remove eel from marinade, reserving marinade. Dry eel slices with paper towels. Sprinkle with salt and pepper and dust lightly with flour.

In a large skillet over medium-high heat, melt butter. Add eel slices and fry on both sides, turning once, until crisp and lightly browned (about 10 minutes total cooking time). Remove from heat. Pour reserved marinade over eel, cover pan immediately, and let stand a few minutes.

To serve, arrange eel slices on a heated platter. Garnish with parsley, olives, and lemon wedges. Pass the sauce (if used).

Serves 4 to 6

PAN AND THE FOODS FROM THE FLOCKS

Pan, The Keeper of the Flocks

Pan, the shepherd god, lover of serenity,
of Orphean song, lover of hills and dales,
a true Hellenist image.
Legends surrounding Pan are many.
Pan, half goat, half man.
Pan *means* all *in Greek,*
and panic was born of him,
as he spread panic when he appeared.
But I prefer to embrace the Greek image,
the child of the earth.
There still hovers over the mountains,
his lament,
singing yet to the shepherds
who guard and walk
the slopes of Greece.
This rascal of Mount Olympus.
And should you hear strange sounds
as you turn your spit,
It is Pan. . . .
Perhaps, you have not added
the right pinch of oregano!

More than two millenia ago in Boeotia ("cow land"), a district northwest of Athens cows roamed the fertile plains in great numbers. But most areas of Greece could not sustain much livestock. During the centuries that followed, wars, erosion, and population increase reduced the grazing land still further. Today the cows in the islands mainly are used to work the fields, and are only rarely slaughtered for the table.

Pork was also a popular meat. Wild boar were there for the hunting, and some farmers managed to rear a few pigs for the table. In The Iliad, Homer records that Achilles hosted Odysseus to a meal of roasted wild pig and goat outside the walls of Ilium (Troy). The contemporary tradition of serving roasted pig for the Christmas feast dates from ancient Greek winter festivals at which suckling pigs were regular fare. Pork in general is not very popular in Greece now, perhaps in part due to the four centuries of Muslim-Turkish rule.

The rocky, barren mountains of Greece are home to the goat, who meanders at will, devouring what little greenery there is. As long ago as 6000 B.C., goats were domesticated for their milk, which was made into cheese. Goat's milk cheese is still extraordinarily popular and the Greeks are generally reluctant to sacrifice the resilient goat, except for a kid to roast at Easter.

To a Greek, meat most often means lamb. The sheep supplies meat, milk, and wool; is content to dine on the sparse scrub; and can negotiate the rocky hills—it is the ideal animal for the ruggedly beautiful terrain of Greece.

Kid and Lamb

In Greece, kid (young goat) is served only for very special occasions. When it comes to everyday meals, lamb is prepared dozens of ways—in stews, grilled on skewers, wrapped and baked with feta and tomatoes, roasted with garlic and herbs, and simmered in tomato sauce with pasta.

Many classic Greek dishes are made with lamb variety meats, all of which are considered great delicacies. Since these meats generally are carried only by specialty butchers, you may need to engage in some culinary detective work to find them. Once you taste these delicious meats, however, your efforts will be amply rewarded.

Kid on a Spit
Katsikaki tis Souvlas

A whole kid or lamb cooked on a spit over hot coals is an Easter tradition. If you have never tasted kid, a great pleasure awaits you. The meat is tender and succulent, with the texture of veal. And the aroma of the thyme used in this recipe will bring the fragrance of the Greek countryside to your table. Don't roast the kid in the oven, for you will deprive yourself of the romance of tending it over the coals. Look for a Greek or Italian butcher from whom you can order the dressed whole kid in advance. For best results marinate the kid 24 hours.

1 kid (9 to 10 lb), dressed
Salt and freshly ground pepper, to taste
4 cloves garlic, crushed
3 tablespoons minced fresh oregano
1 teaspoon minced fresh thyme
2 cups dry white wine
2 cups olive oil
Parsley sprigs, for garnish

Rinse kid with cold water and dry well with paper towels. Rub with salt, pepper, and garlic. In a bowl whisk together oregano, thyme, wine, and oil. Place kid in glass vessel and rub well with some of the oil mixture. Pour remaining oil mixture over kid, cover with plastic wrap, and refrigerate 24 hours, turning occasionally.

Prepare a charcoal fire, preferably in a hooded barbecue with an electrically rotated spit. Remove kid from marinade, reserving marinade. Impale kid on spit; tie front legs and then back legs together securely. When coals are ready, begin cooking the kid, rotating the spit constantly and basting often with reserved marinade. When kid is evenly browned (about 30 minutes), cover loosely with aluminum foil and continue to rotate over coals 1 to 1½ hours.

Remove aluminum foil and continue cooking, basting lavishly, until kid is beautifully browned and tender when pierced with a fork. Total cooking time should be about 3 hours, depending on size of kid and heat of coals.

Remove kid from spit and let rest 20 minutes before carving. Serve on a large platter or wooden board, garnished with clusters of parsley.

Serves 8

Lamb Broth and Shanks
Zomos Arniou

🔲🔲🔲🔲🔲🔲🔲🔲🔲🔲🔲🔲🔲🔲🔲🔲🔲🔲🔲🔲🔲🔲🔲🔲🔲🔲🔲🔲🔲

Slow-simmered lamb shanks and vegetables create a flavorful broth that needs only a splash of lemon juice at the table. The shanks become the second course—accompany with tender young dandelion greens tossed with vinaigrette, a plate of feta, and chilled white retsina.

> 4 medium (about 1 lb each) lamb
>   shanks
> 2 bay leaves
> 4 medium onions, sliced
> 5 or 6 stalks celery
> 2 carrots, cut up
> Salt and freshly ground pepper, to taste
> Lemon wedges, for accompaniment

Place lamb shanks in a large, heavy-bottomed stockpot. Add bay leaves, onions, celery, carrots, and water to cover. Bring to a boil and skim off any foam that forms on surface. Cover, reduce heat, and simmer until lamb is very tender (about 2 hours).

Remove lamb shanks to a heated platter and keep warm. Strain broth, return to stockpot, reheat, and adjust seasoning with salt and pepper. Serve broth with lemon wedges as a first course; follow with the lamb shanks.

Serves 4 as a first course and entrée

Roast Leg of Lamb
Arni Psito

🔲🔲🔲🔲🔲🔲🔲🔲🔲🔲🔲🔲🔲🔲🔲🔲🔲🔲🔲🔲🔲🔲🔲🔲🔲🔲🔲🔲🔲🔲

This classic method of roasting a leg of lamb is pure simplicity. I break with tradition on one point, however. Most Greeks make small slits in the lamb leg and insert slivers of garlic into them. I prefer to rub the crushed garlic on the meat so that the flavor of garlic infuses the pan juices as the lamb cooks. When the lamb is carved, the slice is unmarked and full of fragrance. Note that the lamb should marinate overnight.

> 1 leg of lamb (5 to 6 lb)
> Salt and freshly ground pepper, to taste
> 3 cloves garlic, crushed
> 1 tablespoon minced fresh oregano
> ½ tablespoon minced fresh thyme
> Juice of 1 lemon
> ½ cup olive oil
> 1½ cups dry white wine
> ½ cup butter, melted and cooled

Rinse lamb with cold water and dry well with paper towels. Place in a glass or ceramic vessel. Season with salt and pepper. Rub entire surface of leg with garlic, oregano, and thyme. Sprinkle with lemon juice and pour oil and 1 cup of the wine over the top. Turn leg to coat well on all sides, cover with plastic wrap, and refrigerate overnight, turning occasionally.

Preheat oven to 350° F. Remove lamb from marinade and place in roasting pan. If desired, insert a meat thermometer in the thickest part of the leg. Combine butter and the remaining wine

Continued—

to use as a basting liquid. Roast, basting frequently, about 1½ hours for rare to medium-rare meat (an internal temperature of 130° to 145° F).

Remove from oven and transfer lamb to cutting board. Cover loosely with aluminum foil and let rest 10 minutes. Pour pan juices into a small saucepan; skim off as much fat from surface as possible, heat, and adjust seasoning. Carve lamb and arrange on a warmed platter. Serve pan juices in a bowl alongside.

Serves 6

Leg of Lamb in Foil
Arni à la Pallakari

*This dish is named for the *pallakari*, the brave Greek insurgents who launched the revolution against the Turks in 1821. Serve this patriotic dish with Celery Hearts in Egg-Lemon Sauce (see page 61) and Potatoes Browned in Butter (see page 60).

> *1 leg of lamb (4 to 5 lb)*
> *Salt and freshly ground pepper, to taste*
> *2 cloves garlic, minced*
> *½ cup plus 3 tablespoons butter, plus*
> *   melted butter, for foil*
> *2 pounds small (about 1 in. in diameter)*
> *   white onions, parboiled 10 minutes*
> *   and drained*
> *2 tablespoons each chopped fresh parsley*
> *   and mint*
> *¾ cup dry white wine*
> *½ cup olive oil, plus olive oil for roasting pan*
> *Juice of 2 lemons*
> *1 tablespoon minced fresh oregano*
> *Watercress sprigs, tomato halves, and*
> *   Kalamata olives, for garnish*

Preheat oven to 375° F. Rinse lamb with cold water and pat dry with paper towels. Rub with salt, pepper, and garlic. Set aside.

In a large, deep skillet, melt the ½ cup butter. Brown lamb leg gently on all sides until golden. Remove lamb from pan; strain and reserve butter.

In the same skillet over medium heat, melt 3 tablespoons butter. Add onions, parsley, mint, salt, and pepper; sauté until onions are golden brown on all sides (about 7 minutes). Set aside in pan.

Ready a double-thick sheet of aluminum foil large enough to enclose lamb completely. Brush foil with melted butter and place lamb leg in center. Surround lamb with onions. Brush lamb and onions with reserved strained butter and butter from sautéing onions. Bring ends and edges of foil up around lamb to form a boat. Drizzle lamb with wine, the ½ cup oil, and lemon juice; sprinkle with oregano. Fold foil closed over lamb and seal securely.

Oil a roasting pan. Place lamb in pan and roast 3 hours.

To serve, place wrapped lamb on a large platter. Surround with watercress and tomato halves topped with olives. Unwrap lamb at the table.

Serves 4 or 5

Lamb Shoulder Stuffed with Eggplant

Arni Yemisto me Melitzana

Eggplant is paired with lamb in scores of classic Greek dishes. In this dish minted eggplant is rolled up in a lamb shoulder.

1 medium (about 1 lb) eggplant
Salt and freshly ground pepper, to taste
½ cup plus 2 tablespoons olive oil, or as
    needed
1 medium onion, grated
1 clove garlic, crushed
1 tablespoon each minced fresh mint
    and parsley
1 shoulder of lamb (about 4 lb), boned
1 cup dry white wine
1 to 2 tablespoons freshly squeezed
    lemon juice
½ lemon
8 small new potatoes, peeled
Minced fresh oregano, to taste

Preheat oven to 450° F. Peel eggplant and cut crosswise in thin slices. Season slices on both sides with salt and pepper. In a medium skillet over medium-high heat, warm ¼ cup of the oil. Fry eggplant on both sides until lightly browned and almost tender, adding oil to pan as needed to prevent sticking. Remove eggplant to paper towels to drain.

In a small skillet over medium-high heat, warm the 2 tablespoons oil. Add onion, garlic, mint, and parsley and sauté until onion is translucent (about 5 minutes). Set aside.

Place shoulder of lamb flat on a wooden board. Spread onion mixture over lamb. Season with salt and pepper and arrange eggplant slices evenly on top. Roll lamb from narrow end into a tight cylinder; tie with kitchen twine in several places.

Place rolled lamb in a roasting pan. If desired, insert a meat thermometer in thickest part of roast. Pour ½ cup of the wine over lamb. In a small bowl combine lemon juice and the remaining ¼ cup oil to use for basting. Spear base of half lemon on the end of a fork to use as a baster.

Roast lamb 15 minutes, then reduce oven heat to 300° F. Continue roasting, basting frequently, 1 hour and 45 minutes for rare to medium-rare meat (an internal temperature of 130° to 145° F).

While lamb is roasting, parboil potatoes in water to cover 15 minutes; drain. About 30 minutes before lamb is ready, add potatoes to pan; sprinkle lightly with salt, pepper, and oregano and baste with pan juices.

Remove lamb from oven and transfer to a cutting board. Cover loosely with aluminum foil and let rest 10 minutes. Transfer potatoes to a covered container to keep warm. Pour pan juices into a small saucepan; skim off as much fat from surface as possible. Add the remaining wine and season with salt and pepper. Simmer over low heat several minutes.

To serve, remove and discard string from lamb and cut roll in 1-inch-thick slices. Arrange slices on a heated platter and surround with potatoes. Pour pan juices into a bowl and serve alongside.

Serves 6

Stuffed Crown of Lamb

Arnaki Yemisto

Ask your butcher to cut through the backbone between the ribs before tying the rack into a crown. This will make the elegant rack of lamb much easier to carve. Note that you need to cook the rice before you can prepare the stuffing.

Rice Stuffing (see following recipe)
1 tablespoon minced fresh oregano
2 cloves garlic, minced
2 tablespoons olive oil
1 crown of lamb (18-rib rack)
½ cup dry white wine

Prepare stuffing and set aside. Preheat oven to 400° F.

In a small bowl mix together oregano, garlic, and oil. Rub mixture over entire surface of lamb. Cover rib tips with aluminum foil. Place lamb in roasting pan and pour wine over lamb. If desired, insert a meat thermometer in thickest part of roast. Roast 25 minutes.

Remove lamb from oven and reduce oven heat to 350° F. Pack stuffing into crown. Roast 1 hour more for rare to medium-rare meat (an internal temperature of 130° to 145° F).

Remove lamb from oven and transfer to a cutting board. Cover loosely with aluminum foil and let stand 10 minutes. Place on a heated platter. Carve into chops at the table. Serve each guest 3 chops and a large spoonful of the stuffing.

Serves 6

Rice Stuffing

½ cup butter
3 green onions, minced
1 clove garlic, minced
2 tablespoons chopped fresh parsley
2 cups cooked long-grain white rice
¼ cup pine nuts
Salt and freshly ground pepper, to taste

In a skillet over medium heat, melt butter. Add onions, garlic, and parsley; sauté until onions are translucent (about 5 minutes). Add rice and nuts; toss well and heat gently to blend flavors. Season with salt and pepper.

Lamb on Skewers
Arni Souvlakia

*S*ouvlakia, the skewered meat that is found throughout Greece, is an adaptation of the old Turkish custom of impaling meat on a sword and roasting it over a fire. In Greece cooks insist on seasoning their souvlakia with oregano, but not just any oregano will do. *Origanum dubium*, a more strongly flavored variety than the ubiquitous *Origanum vulgare*, is preferred. Note that the meat should marinate several hours or overnight.

> 2 medium onions
> 3 green bell peppers
> 1 leg of lamb (4 to 5 lb), boned and cut
>   in 1½-inch cubes
> 1 tablespoon minced fresh oregano
> ½ cup olive oil
> 3 bay leaves
> 3 cloves garlic, minced
> Juice of 2 lemons
> 1 cup dry white wine
> Salt and freshly ground pepper, to taste
> 6 firm, ripe tomatoes, quartered

Cut onions in quarters and separate layers. Cut peppers in quarters, remove ribs and seeds, and cut each quarter in half crosswise.

In a large, shallow flameproof baking dish, combine all ingredients except tomatoes. Mix thoroughly so that meat is well coated with marinade. Cover and refrigerate several hours or overnight.

Preheat broiler. Add tomato wedges to marinade and mix gently to coat. Thread meat cubes on 6 metal skewers, alternating them with onion, pepper, and tomato pieces. Lay filled skewers in baking dish and turn several times in marinade.

Remove filled skewers, place a rack in baking dish, and lay skewers on rack. Broil about 4 inches from heat, turning several times and basting with marinade from pan, until lamb is browned and cooked to your liking (about 20 minutes for rosy lamb).

Serve each guest 1 skewer. Pour hot marinade from pan into a small bowl and pass at the table.

Serves 6

Cephalonian Meat Pie

Kreatopita

*T*here are many variations on this meat pie, named for the large, hilly Ionian island, known as Cephalonia or Kefallinia, that is the ancestral homeland of many Greek immigrants to North America. Read the tips on working with filo dough (see page 14) before beginning the recipe.

¼ cup butter, plus 1 cup melted butter
*   for filo*
3 pounds lean lamb, cut in ½-inch dice
Salt and freshly ground pepper, to taste
2 cups diced potato (½-in. dice)
1½ cups minced onion
1 cup minced celery
½ cup minced fresh parsley
2 cloves garlic, minced
1 teaspoon ground cinnamon
½ teaspoon dried mint, crushed
4 hard-cooked eggs, cut in ½-inch dice
½ cup cooked long-grain white rice
½ cup olive oil
1 cup crumbled feta cheese
1 pound filo dough, thawed overnight in
*   refrigerator if frozen*

In a large skillet over medium heat, melt the ¼ cup butter. Add lamb and sprinkle with salt and pepper. Sauté until lightly browned (about 5 minutes), then transfer to a large mixing bowl. Add remaining ingredients except filo and melted butter. Mix well and adjust seasoning.

Preheat oven to 350° F. Brush a 9- by 13-inch baking dish with melted butter. Unfold filo dough so it lays flat, then cover to prevent it from drying out. Line dish with about half of the filo sheets, brushing each with melted butter before adding the next sheet. Spread lamb mixture evenly over filo in dish. Cover with remaining filo sheets, brushing each with butter as you layer it in the dish. Lavishly brush top sheet with butter. With a very sharp knife or single-edged razor blade, cut in large squares, going only deep enough to reach through the unfilled top filo layers.

Bake until lightly browned and crispy (about 1 hour). Remove from oven, cool slightly, then cut in squares to serve.

Serves 8 to 12

Lamb with Yogurt

Arni me Yiaourti

To my mind, this is among the very finest of the many Greek lamb dishes. Have your butcher bone the rack, leaving the eye of the rib in one strip. Take the bones with you; they won't be served, but they will be used to enrich the sauce.

2 teaspoons minced fresh oregano
1 teaspoon minced fresh thyme
1 clove garlic, crushed
1 rack of lamb (6 or 9 chops), boned
*   with eye of rib in single piece, bones*
*   reserved*
Salt and freshly ground pepper, to taste
Juice of 2 lemons
Dash brandy
Yogurt Sauce (see following recipe)

Preheat oven to 500° F. In a small bowl, combine oregano, thyme, and garlic; rub thoroughly over lamb. Season with salt and pepper and rub with lemon juice. Place lamb meat and rib bones on a rack in a roasting pan. Sprinkle meat with brandy. Roast until tender but still quite pink (about 15 minutes).

While meat is cooking, prepare sauce. Remove meat from oven and transfer to a cutting board. Cover loosely with aluminum foil and let rest 5 minutes. Pour off pan juices into a small bowl and skim off as much fat from surface as possible.

Slice meat thinly and arrange on a heated platter. Add pan juices to Yogurt Sauce and serve in a bowl alongside.

Serves 2 or 3

Yogurt Sauce
1 cup plain yogurt
1 tablespoon flour
2 tablespoons water
Dash brandy
Pan juices

Place yogurt and pan juices in a small saucepan over very low heat. Stir flour into the water and add to pan. Add brandy and mix well. Cook very slowly 15 minutes.

Baked Lamb Steaks and Artichokes

Arni me Anginares

*S*poon a row of Rice and Fides Pilaf (see page 66) on the serving platter with the lamb steaks and artichokes. Make up a plate of feta cheese and olives to accompany the main course. Serve fresh fruit to end the meal.

6 medium artichokes
Juice of 3 lemons
Salt, to taste
½ cup olive oil
3 cloves garlic, minced
½ cup chopped fresh parsley
1 tablespoon minced fresh oregano
2 tablespoons tomato paste
½ cup water
4 ripe tomatoes, peeled and chopped
1 cup white wine
6 lamb steaks (about 6 oz each)
Freshly ground pepper, to taste

Preheat oven to 375° F. Remove 3 or 4 outer layers of leaves from artichokes. Slice 1 inch off leaf tops and trim stems. Cut artichokes in half lengthwise and remove thistles with a spoon. Rub artichokes with one third of lemon juice and let stand 15 minutes. Bring a saucepan filled with water to a boil. Add artichokes and salt and parboil 15 minutes; drain and set aside.

In a skillet over medium-high heat, warm oil. Add garlic, parsley, and oregano and sauté until garlic is translucent (about 5 minutes). Dilute tomato paste in the water and add to skillet with the remaining lemon juice, tomatoes, and wine. Simmer, uncovered, 10 minutes.

Select a baking dish in which lamb steaks will fit side by side. Arrange steaks in a row on one side of dish. Place artichokes in a row alongside. Season with salt and pepper. Pour tomato mixture over steaks and artichokes. Bake until tender (about 40 minutes).

To serve, arrange steaks in a line on a heated platter. Place artichokes in a line alongside them. Spoon sauce over the top.

Serves 6

Baked Lamb Shanks

Podarakia Arniou

Lamb shanks require long, slow cooking, so plan your kitchen schedule accordingly. They are done when the meat begins to fall away from the bone. Serve these lamb shanks with salad greens tossed with cucumber and tomato and a fine red wine.

4 lamb shanks (about 1 lb each)
Salt and freshly ground pepper, to taste
2 cloves garlic, minced
2 small carrots, thinly sliced lengthwise
1 large onion, thinly sliced
2 stalks celery, halved crosswise and then
    thinly sliced lengthwise
2 bay leaves, crushed
1 tablespoon minced fresh oregano or
    1 teaspoon dried oregano, crumbled
½ tablespoon minced fresh thyme or
    ½ teaspoon dried thyme, crumbled
2 cups Basic Tomato Sauce (see page 178)
1 cup white wine
½ cup olive oil
8 to 12 small new potatoes (optional)

Preheat oven to 375° F. Place lamb shanks in a roasting pan. Rub well on all sides with salt, pepper, and garlic. Tuck carrots, onion, celery, and bay leaves around shanks. Sprinkle with oregano and thyme. Combine tomato sauce, wine, and oil; pour over shanks.

Cover pan and bake, basting occasionally with sauce, until meat easily pulls away from bone (about 2 hours). During last 30 minutes of cooking, uncover pan and increase oven temperature to 400° F. If desired, add potatoes at this point, basting them with pan sauces.

To serve, arrange shanks on a heated platter and surround with potatoes (if used). Pour pan sauce over shanks.

Serves 4

Lamb Shanks in Foil

Arni sto Harti

GGGGGGGGGGGGGGGGGGGGGGGGGGGGGGGGGGGGGGGGGGGGGGGGGGGGGGGGGGGGGGGGGGGGGGGG

*A*ccompany this hearty lamb shank dish with a green salad, thick slices of feta, Potatoes Browned in Butter (see page 60), and a rosé retsina.

4 lamb shanks (about 1 lb each)
Butter, for browning
2 cloves garlic, minced
1 can (16 oz) plum tomatoes, drained
    and chopped
1 carrot, thinly sliced
1 onion, thinly sliced
½ cup olive oil, plus olive oil for baking
    pan
2 teaspoons minced fresh oregano or
    ½ teaspoon dried oregano, crumbled
½ cup dry white wine
Salt and freshly ground pepper, to taste

Preheat oven to 375° F. In a dutch oven or large skillet over medium heat, melt butter. Add lamb shanks and half of the garlic and brown shanks well on all sides. Remove shanks to paper towels to drain.

Ready 4 double-thick sheets of aluminum foil, each large enough to enclose securely 1 lamb shank. Place 1 shank on each sheet. Mix together the remaining garlic, tomatoes, carrot, onion, ½ cup olive oil, oregano, wine, salt, and pepper. Bring ends and edges of foil up around lamb. Arrange an equal amount of the carrot mixture on top of each shank. Close foil packets securely, crimping edges tightly.

Oil a baking pan and place packets in it. Bake until shanks are tender, 1½ to 2 hours. Serve packets on individual plates for guests to open.

Serves 4

Lamb, Bandit Style
Arni Kleftiko

During the four centuries that the Ottoman Empire ruled Greece, many Greeks hid in the mountains like bandits, striking out against the Turks when they could. In order to prevent their being detected, they cooked their meat by burying it with hot stones. The meat roasted beautifully, and no cooking smoke rose to be seen by the enemy. Roasting foods in aluminum foil is a modern adaptation of this guerilla cuisine.

*2 pounds boneless lean lamb,
    cut in 1½-inch cubes*
*½ cup olive oil, plus olive oil for brushing
    foil and baking pan*
1 clove garlic, minced
Juice of 1 lemon
1 large onion, minced
⅓ to ½ cup dry sherry
1½ tablespoons minced fresh oregano
Salt and freshly ground pepper, to taste
1 large ripe tomato, cut in 6 slices
¾ cup crumbled feta cheese
3 tablespoons butter, cut in 6 pats

Preheat oven to 375° F. In a large bowl mix together lamb, the ½ cup oil, garlic, lemon juice, onion, sherry, 1 tablespoon of the oregano, salt, and pepper.

Ready 6 double-thick sheets of aluminum foil, each large enough to enclose securely one sixth of the meat mixture. Brush aluminum foil with oil. Arrange an equal amount of the meat mixture in center of each sheet, bringing up edges of foil to trap liquid. Top each portion with a tomato slice, then some feta cheese. Sprinkle with remaining oregano. Place a butter pat on top of portion and close foil packet securely, crimping edges tightly.

Oil a baking pan and place packets in it. Bake 45 minutes to 1 hour. Serve packets on individual plates for guests to open.

Serves 6

Lamb with Kritharaki

Arni Giouvetsi

Kritharaki is a rice-shaped pasta that is usually added to soups and casseroles. Italian *orzo* is similar in size and shape and may be substituted. Serve each guest a shallow soup bowl with a mound of the kritharaki and one sixth of the lamb. Accompany with Boiled Greens with Lemon Juice and Olive Oil (see page 61).

2 pounds boneless lamb from leg or
   shoulder, cut in 1½-inch cubes
1 onion, sliced
2 cloves garlic, minced
Minced fresh oregano, to taste
Salt and freshly ground pepper, to taste
6 tablespoons butter
½ cup dry white wine
1 pound kritharaki pasta
3 cups water
1 cup Basic Tomato Sauce (see page 178)
Freshly grated kefalotyri or Parmesan
   cheese, for accompaniment

Preheat oven to 450° F. In a baking pan combine lamb, onion, and garlic. Season with oregano, salt, and pepper. Melt 2 tablespoons of the butter and drizzle over the top.

Place in oven until meat and onion are lightly browned (about 20 minutes). Add wine and cook 15 minutes, basting frequently with pan juices. Reduce oven heat to 350° F and bake until meat is very tender and browned (about 30 minutes).

While meat is cooking, bring a large saucepan filled with water to a boil. Add kritharaki and parboil 5 minutes; drain and set aside.

Remove meat from pan and keep warm. Add the 3 cups water, tomato sauce, and the remaining butter to baking pan. Adjust seasoning with salt and pepper. Return to oven and bring to a boil.

Slowly add kritharaki to baking pan, stir well, and bake until pasta is the consistency of cooked rice (about 20 minutes).

Serve lamb and pasta in shallow soup bowls. Pass the cheese.

Serves 6

Lamb in Tomato Sauce with Macaroni
Arni Kapama

GGGGGGGGGGGGGGGGGGGGGGGGGGGGGGGGGGGGGGGGGGGGGGGGGGGGGGGGGGGGGGGGGGGGGGGGGG

Kapama is a classic style of braising lamb, beef, or chicken with onions, tomatoes, and cinnamon. Here the savory stew is presented with a platter of cheese-laced macaroni.

¼ cup butter
*2 pounds boneless lamb stew meat, cut
   in 1½-inch cubes*
Salt and freshly ground pepper, to taste
2 cloves garlic, minced
2 onions, chopped
2 bay leaves
*1 cinnamon stick (about 2 in. long),
   broken in half*
Dash each ground cinnamon and cloves
*1 can (16 oz) plum tomatoes, chopped,
   with their liquid*
*1 cup each Basic Tomato Sauce (see
   page 178) and dry white wine*
Athenian Macaroni (see page 71)
*Freshly grated kefalotyri or Parmesan
   cheese, for sprinkling*

In a dutch oven over medium heat, melt butter. Add lamb and season with salt and pepper; sauté until lightly browned (about 5 minutes). Add garlic and onions and sauté until onions are translucent (about 5 minutes). Stir in bay leaves, cinnamon stick, ground cinnamon, cloves, tomatoes and liquid, tomato sauce, and wine. Mix well, cover, and simmer over low heat, stirring occasionally, until lamb is tender (about 1 hour). Add a little water if lamb is not completely immersed.

Meanwhile, prepare macaroni, timing it so that it is ready when lamb is tender. Spoon some of the sauce from lamb over the top. Transfer cooked macaroni to serving platter.

With a slotted utensil transfer lamb to a heated platter. Pour the remaining sauce from dutch oven into a bowl and place alongside with the macaroni. Pass the cheese.

Serves 6

***Beef Pot Roast in Tomato Sauce With Maca-
roni (Vothino Kapama)*** Substitute one 3-pound beef chuck or round roast for lamb. Sliver garlic cloves and quarter onions. Increase butter to ½ cup and brown beef roast. Add onions and garlic, but do not sauté. Proceed as directed, adding 1 teaspoon ground allspice and 1 cup chopped celery with the cinnamon, and substituting red wine for the white wine; add water if beef is not completely immersed. Cook until tender (about 2 hours). Prepare and dress macaroni as directed. Slice roast and arrange on a heated platter with remaining sauce and cheese alongside.

Lamb Stew

Arni Yahni

GGGGGGGGGGGGGGGGGGGGGGGGGGGGGGGGGGGGGGGGGGGGGGGGGGGGGGGGGGGGGGGGGGGGGGGGGGG

*L*amb stew is a basic recipe that undergoes countless variations, depending upon which vegetables are in season (see following recipes). The slow browning of the meat and onions is the secret to the success of this dish.

> *3 tablespoons butter*
> *2 pounds boneless lamb stew meat, cut*
> *in 1½-inch cubes*
> *3 medium onions, chopped*
> *1 clove garlic, minced*
> *1 tablespoon chopped fresh parsley*
> *Salt and freshly ground pepper, to taste*
> *¾ cup tomato paste*
> *2 cups water*
> *1 cup dry white wine*

In a dutch oven over medium heat, melt butter. Add lamb, onions, garlic, parsley, salt, and pepper. Gently cook until lamb and onions are delicately browned on all sides (about 8 minutes).

Dilute tomato paste in the water and add to skillet with wine; stir well and reduce heat. Simmer until meat is tender (about 1 hour), adding a little water if needed to keep the meat immersed.

Serves 6

Lamb Stew With Artichokes (Arni Yahni me Anginares) Remove 3 or 4 outer layers of leaves from 6 medium artichokes. Slice 1 inch off leaf tops and trim stems. Cut artichokes in half lengthwise and scoop out thistles with a spoon. Rub artichokes with juice of 1 lemon. In a skillet over medium heat, melt 2 to 3 tablespoons butter. Add artichokes, sprinkle with minced fresh dill to taste, and brown gently. Add to stew 20 to 30 minutes before end of cooking. Simmer until tender.

Lamb Stew With Cauliflower (Arni Yahni me Kounopedi Fresko) Cut 1 medium head (about 1 pound) cauliflower in florets. In a skillet over medium heat, melt 2 tablespoons butter. Add florets and brown gently on all sides. Add to stew 10 to 15 minutes before end of cooking. Simmer until tender.

Lamb Stew With Green Beans (Arni Yahni me Fassoulakia Freska) Trim ends and remove strings from 1½ pounds green beans; snap in half or cut lengthwise in thin slices. Bring a saucepan of water to a boil and parboil beans 5 minutes. Drain and add to stew 10 to 20 minutes before end of cooking, depending upon cut; simmer until tender.

Lamb Stew With Okra (Arni Yahni me Bamyes) Trim and discard stems from 1½ pounds okra, but do not pierce pods. Place in a bowl and squeeze juice of 1 lemon over top. Toss to mix. Add to stew about 20 minutes before end of cooking. Stir gently, being careful not to break up okra, and simmer until tender.

Continued—

Lamb Stew With Peas (Arni Yahni me Bizelia) Add 3 cups shelled peas (about 3 pounds unshelled) to stew about 10 minutes before end of cooking. Simmer until tender. Garnish with minced fresh mint before serving.

Lamb Stew With Potatoes (Arni Yahni me Patates) Peel 12 small potatoes. In a skillet over medium heat, melt 2 to 3 tablespoons butter. Add potatoes and brown gently on all sides. Add to stew 20 to 30 minutes before end of cooking. Simmer until tender. Garnish stew with minced fresh parsley.

Lamb Stew With Zucchini (Arni Yahni me Kolokithia) Trim ends from 2 pounds small zucchini. Cut zucchini in half lengthwise. In a skillet over medium heat, melt 2 tablespoons butter. Add zucchini and brown gently. Add to stew 10 to 15 minutes before end of cooking. Simmer until tender.

Lamb Kidney Omelet

Avga me Nafra

In Greek cooking there are no reservations when it comes to eggs. Our sauces are blended with eggs, our breads are brushed with eggs, and our baked macaroni dishes are bound with eggs. Plus, at a moment's notice a Greek will willingly cook up an omelet, such as this delectable lamb kidney dish.

6 lamb kidneys
5 tablespoons butter
4 green onions, finely chopped
2 tablespoons minced fresh parsley
Salt and freshly ground pepper, to taste
1 teaspoon minced fresh oregano
Dry white wine
1 tablespoon tomato paste
8 eggs, beaten

Pull off and discard outer membrane of kidneys. Trim away any fat and connective tissue. Cut kidneys crosswise in thin slices.

In a skillet over medium heat, melt 2 tablespoons of the butter. Add kidneys, onions, and parsley and sauté briskly 3 minutes. Sprinkle with salt, pepper, and oregano, and add a splash of wine. Reduce heat and cook 2 to 3 minutes. Add tomato paste to skillet and stir well; remove from heat and keep warm.

In a large omelet pan or skillet over medium heat, melt the remaining butter. Pour eggs into pan, tilting pan to distribute eggs evenly and shaking pan to keep eggs from sticking. Reduce heat slightly; lift edges of omelet with a spatula to allow uncooked egg to flow underneath. When eggs are almost cooked but still creamy on top, place kidney mixture in a line down center. Fold omelet sides over filling and cook 1 or 2 minutes longer.

Carefully slide omelet onto a heated platter and serve.

Serves 4

Lamb Kidneys on Skewers

Nafra Souvlakia

If you are planning to use bamboo skewers for these kabobs, immerse the skewers in water 30 minutes before threading the kidneys on them. This keeps the bamboo from catching fire.

8 lamb kidneys
Salt and freshly ground pepper, to taste
1 tablespoon minced fresh oregano
1 teaspoon minced fresh thyme
1 clove garlic, minced
½ cup each dry white wine and olive oil
Rice Pilaf (see page 67)
Chopped fresh parsley and lemon
  wedges, for garnish

Pull off and discard outer membrane of kidneys. Trim away any fat and connective tissue. Cut kidneys in half crosswise. Place in a bowl with salt, pepper, oregano, thyme, and garlic. Pour in wine and oil and turn kidneys to coat well. Let stand 30 minutes, turning kidneys several times so they absorb marinade evenly.

While kidneys are marinating, put pilaf on to cook. Preheat broiler.

Remove kidneys from marinade, reserving marinade. Thread 4 kidney halves on each metal skewer or presoaked bamboo skewer. Place on a broiler rack over a drip pan. Position about 4 inches below broiler flame and cook 5 minutes. Turn skewers, baste with reserved marinade, and cook on second side until done but still pink in the center (3 to 4 minutes).

Remove from broiler. Mound pilaf on a warmed serving platter and arrange skewers on top. Sprinkle kidneys with chopped parsley and garnish platter with lemon wedges.

Serves 4

Lamb Kidney Pilaf
Nafra Pilafi

🔲🔲🔲🔲🔲🔲🔲🔲🔲🔲🔲🔲🔲🔲🔲🔲🔲🔲🔲🔲🔲🔲🔲🔲🔲

*T*his combination of lamb kidneys cooked in herbs and wine and served with fluffy pilaf is satisfying fare. It is the perfect dish for the early days of spring, when the blossoms begin to bud and the cold winds cease blowing.

8 lamb kidneys
¼ cup butter
6 green onions, finely chopped
1 clove garlic, minced
2 tablespoons chopped fresh parsley
1 teaspoon dried fines herbes, crushed
1 bay leaf
3 tablespoons tomato paste
½ cup water
1 cup dry white wine or sherry
Rice Pilaf (see page 67)

Pull off and discard outer membrane of kidneys. Trim away any fat and connective tissue. Cut kidneys in half crosswise, then cut each half crosswise in 4 slices.

In a deep skillet over medium heat, melt butter. Add kidneys and sauté until lightly browned (about 3 minutes). Add onions, garlic, parsley, fines herbes, and bay leaf; sauté until onions are translucent (about 5 minutes). Dilute tomato paste in the water and add to pan with wine. Stir well, reduce heat, and simmer 25 minutes.

Pack hot pilaf in individual molds, cool slightly, then unmold on serving plates. Spoon kidneys over rice molds.

Serves 4

Lamb Tongues Vinaigrette
Glossa Arniou Ladoxeidou

🔲🔲🔲🔲🔲🔲🔲🔲🔲🔲🔲🔲🔲🔲🔲🔲🔲🔲🔲🔲🔲🔲🔲🔲🔲

*I*nclude this versatile dish in a large buffet, or serve for a late supper with sliced tomatoes, feta cheese, and Kalamata olives. Note that the tongues require long cooking and then chilling in the dressing.

8 lamb tongues
2 yellow onions, quartered
1 whole bay leaf, plus 1 bay leaf, crushed
2 whole cloves
3 whole cloves garlic, plus 2 cloves garlic, minced
Salt, to taste
½ cup each olive oil, white wine vinegar, and white wine
6 green onions (including some green top), finely chopped
3 tablespoons minced fresh parsley, plus minced parsley for garnish
Minced fresh oregano, to taste
Freshly ground pepper, to taste

Wash tongues under cold water and place in a large saucepan. Add yellow onions, the whole bay leaf, whole cloves, and the 3 cloves garlic. Add water to cover and bring to a boil. Reduce heat and simmer until tongues are tender when pierced with a fork (1 to 1½ hours). Add a little salt toward end of cooking.

Drain tongues and let cool until they can be handled. Pull skin off tongues and trim away any fat. Cut lengthwise in ¼-inch-thick slices.

Continued—

Lamb Tongues Vinaigrette continued—

Arrange cooled tongue slices in a deep platter. Place minced garlic in a small bowl. Add crushed bay leaf, oil, vinegar, wine, green onions, the 3 tablespoons parsley, oregano, and salt and pepper to taste. Whisk together until blended. Pour sauce over tongue slices, garnish with remaining parsley, cover, and chill well before serving.

Serves 4 to 6

Lamb Tongues in Sauce
Glossa Arniou me Saltsa

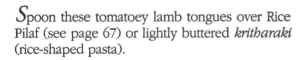

*S*poon these tomatoey lamb tongues over Rice Pilaf (see page 67) or lightly buttered *kritharaki* (rice-shaped pasta).

2 onions, quartered, plus 2 onions,
    grated
8 lamb tongues
1 bay leaf
2 whole cloves
3 whole cloves garlic, plus 1 clove garlic,
    minced
½ cup butter
2 tablespoons chopped fresh parsley
Pinch each dried thyme and oregano,
    crushed
3 ripe tomatoes, peeled and chopped
2 tablespoons tomato paste
½ cup dry white wine

Wash tongues under cold water and place in a large saucepan. Add quartered onions, bay leaf,

cloves, and whole garlic cloves. Add water to cover and bring to a boil. Reduce heat and simmer until tongues are tender when pierced with a fork (1 to 1½ hours). Drain tongues, reserving cooking liquid, and let tongues cool until they can be handled. Pull skin off tongues and trim away any fat. Cut lengthwise in ½-inch-thick slices. Set aside.

In a large skillet over medium heat, melt ¼ cup of the butter. Add grated onions, minced garlic, parsley, thyme, and oregano; sauté until onions are translucent (about 5 minutes). Add tomatoes, tomato paste, wine, and reserved cooking liquid; simmer 15 minutes.

Meanwhile, in another skillet melt the remaining butter over medium heat. Add tongue slices and brown lightly. Transfer to simmering tomato sauce and continue to cook, uncovered, until sauce is very thick (about 30 minutes).

Serves 4 to 6

Lamb Brains Baked with Eggs

Miala sto Fournou

This is a Greek version of a soufflé, and although it lacks the great loft of the French classic, it is delicious nonetheless. If you cannot find lamb brains, calf brains may be substituted.

> *6 whole lamb or calf brains*
> *1 bay leaf*
> *1 onion, quartered*
> *Butter, as needed*
> *Salt and freshly ground pepper, to taste*
> *1 tablespoon each minced fresh oregano and parsley*
> *8 eggs*
> *¼ cup whipping cream*
> *1 tablespoon freshly grated kefalotyri or Parmesan cheese*

Rinse brains in cold water and place in a bowl. Add cold water to cover and let stand 15 minutes.

Drain brains and peel away membrane and connective tissue. Rinse with cold water and place in a saucepan. Add water to cover, bay leaf, and onion. Bring to a boil, reduce heat, and simmer 15 to 20 minutes; drain and rinse under cold water. Cut in 1-inch-thick slices.

Preheat oven to 350° F. Butter a shallow baking dish and arrange sliced brains in bottom. Sprinkle with salt, pepper, oregano, and parsley. In a medium bowl whisk together eggs and cream until very frothy. Pour over brains. Dot with as much butter as desired.

Bake until eggs are set and top is lightly browned (30 to 45 minutes). Cool slightly, then cut in squares. With a spatula transfer to a heated platter.

Serves 6

Lamb Brains in White Sauce
Miala me Aspri Saltsa

GGGGGGGGGGGGGGGGGGGGGGGGGGGGGGGGGGGGG

*A*ccompany this extremely rich dish with a tossed green salad or boiled young greens.

Basic White Sauce (see page 174)
3 whole lamb or calf brains
1 bay leaf
1 onion, quartered
Butter, as needed
Salt and freshly ground pepper, to taste
Juice of 1 lemon
3 tablespoons freshly grated kefalotyri or
  Parmesan cheese

Prepare sauce and set aside. Preheat oven to 350° F.

Rinse brains in cold water and place in a bowl. Add cold water to cover and let stand 15 minutes. Drain; peel away membrane and connective tissue. Rinse with cold water and place in a saucepan. Add water to cover, bay leaf, and onion. Bring to a boil, reduce heat, and simmer 15 to 20 minutes. Drain and rinse under cold water. Cut in ½-inch-thick slices.

Butter a 4- to 6-cup casserole and arrange sliced brains in bottom. Sprinkle with salt, pepper, and lemon juice. Cover with white sauce, dot with butter, and sprinkle with cheese.

Bake until top is nicely browned and brains are very tender when pierced with a fork (30 to 45 minutes).

Serves 4

Fried Lamb Brains
Miala Tighanita

GGGGGGGGGGGGGGGGGGGGGGGGGGGGGGGGGGGGGGG

*F*or best results, chill the brains before slicing them. This will help them to hold their shape better as they fry.

4 whole lamb or calf brains
2 bay leaves
1 onion, quartered
Salt and freshly ground pepper, to taste
Flour, for dusting
2 egg yolks
Butter, for panfrying
Chopped fresh parsley and lemon
  wedges, for garnish

Rinse brains in cold water and place in a bowl. Add cold water to cover and let stand 15 minutes. Drain; peel away membrane and connective tissue. Rinse with cold water and place in a saucepan. Add water to cover, bay leaf, and onion. Bring to a boil, reduce heat, and simmer 15 to 20 minutes. Drain and rinse under cold water. Cover and chill; cut in ½-inch-thick slices.

Season sliced brains with salt and pepper. Place flour in a shallow bowl. In a second bowl, beat egg yolks lightly.

In a skillet over medium heat, melt butter. Dust brain slices in flour, then dip in egg. Fry in butter on both sides until golden brown (about 5 minutes total cooking time). Remove to a heated platter. Sprinkle with parsley and garnish with lemon wedges. Serve immediately.

Serves 4

Veal, Beef, and Pork

GGGGGGGGGGGGGGGGGGGGGGGGGGGGGGGGGGGGGGGGGGGGGGGGGGGGGGGGGGGGGGGGGG

Veal is rarely served in Greece. It is very difficult to find, and expensive when you manage to find it. Because of veal's greater availability in the United States, Greek Americans have created dishes to showcase it.

Beef and pork dishes are also more regularly found on the tables of immigrants to North America than they are in the Greek islands, although Greek winter meals sometimes feature a beef stew with tomatoes and pearl onions or a platter of boiled beef with carrots, potatoes, and leeks.

Veal Chops with White Sauce
Mosharaki me Aspri Saltsa

GGGGGGGGGGGGGGGGGGGGGGGGGGGGGGGGGGGGGGGGGGGGGGGGGGGGGGGGGGGGGGGGGG

This eggplant-and-veal combination is an exquisite presentation, with extraordinary flavor to match. Begin the meal with Chilled Chicken Soup With Egg-Lemon Sauce (see page 173), then serve the veal chops with a green salad and a bottle of the finest white retsina.

Basic White Sauce (see page 174)
1 small eggplant
Salt and freshly ground pepper, to taste
Olive oil, for broiling
4 veal chops (about 5 oz each), boned
1 clove garlic, minced
Butter, for sautéing
1½ tablespoons brandy
Freshly grated kefalotyri or Parmesan
*   cheese, to taste*

Prepare sauce and set aside. Preheat broiler. Trim ends from eggplant; cut eggplant lengthwise in four ¼-inch-thick slices. Season slices with salt and pepper and brush with oil. Arrange on a broiler pan and broil, turning once, until just tender and golden on both sides (about 6 minutes total cooking time). Remove to paper towels to drain.

Lightly pound veal chops with a wooden mallet until about ¼ inch thick. Rub chops with garlic, salt, and pepper. In a skillet over medium-high heat, melt butter. Add veal and fry quickly on both sides until done to taste; do not overcook.

Transfer chops to a flameproof baking dish, arranging them in a single layer. Place an eggplant slice on top of each chop. Stir brandy into reserved white sauce; adjust seasoning. Pour sauce over chops and sprinkle with cheese.

Slip baking dish under broiler. Broil until sauce is golden and bubbly (about 5 minutes). Serve immediately.

Serves 4

Veal Birds with Artichokes Evoula
Mosharaki me Anginares

Many Greek cookbooks published in the United States include recipes for veal birds. In my own research on classic Greek cuisine I have found no reference to them, but I have decided to join with my fellow Greek-American cooks. Here is my recipe for veal birds stuffed with artichoke hearts.

12 small artichokes (about 2 in. in
    diameter)
12 veal scallops (about 3 oz each)
⅓ cup plus 3 tablespoons butter
2 bunches (about 12) green onions,
    finely chopped
3 tablespoons finely chopped fresh
    parsley
1 clove garlic, finely chopped
2 cups Basic Tomato Sauce (see page 178)
Salt and freshly ground pepper, to taste
2 tablespoons flour
2 tablespoons water
1¼ cups dry sherry

Remove outer layers of leaves from artichokes until you reach inner, tender heart leaves. Slice off thorny leaf tips and trim stems. Bring a large pot of water to a boil, add artichokes, and cook until tender when pierced with a fork (20 to 30 minutes). Drain and cool. Cut in half, remove any fuzzy choke, then chop hearts; reserve.

Lightly pound veal scallops with a wooden mallet until they are about ⅛ inch thick; set aside.

Preheat oven to 350° F. In a skillet over medium heat, melt the 3 tablespoons butter. Add onions, parsley, garlic, and reserved hearts; sauté until onions are translucent (about 5 minutes). Add ¼ cup of the tomato sauce, salt, and pepper. Dissolve flour in the water and add to skillet. Mix well and simmer, stirring, 5 minutes. Add ¼ cup of the sherry and stir well. Remove from heat and cool slightly.

Place an equal portion of the artichoke mixture in the center of each veal scallop. Roll up into tight cylinders and secure with toothpicks.

In a large skillet over medium heat, melt the ⅓ cup butter. Add veal rolls and gently brown on all sides. Remove rolls and place, side by side, in a heavy casserole. Pour butter from skillet over rolls. In a small bowl, mix together the remaining tomato sauce and the remaining sherry; pour over rolls. Sprinkle lightly with salt and pepper.

Bake until veal is tender (30 to 45 minutes). Remove rolls to a heated platter and spoon sauce over top.

Serves 6

Beef Stew with Onions
Stefado

The term *stefado* is used for a meat or poultry stew that contains lots of onions and garlic and is seasoned with vinegar. My version departs from tradition by using red wine in place of vinegar. Some cooks add walnut halves and cubes of feta at the last minute.

*Olive oil or butter, for browning meat
    and onions*
*3 pounds beef chuck or top round, cut in
    2-inch cubes*
3 cloves garlic, chopped
3 bay leaves
*1 cinnamon stick (about 2 in. long),
    broken in half*
1 teaspoon ground allspice
¾ cup tomato paste
1 cup water
1½ cups full-bodied red wine
3 pounds small white onions, peeled

In a dutch oven over high heat, warm oil. Add beef and brown well on all sides. Add garlic, bay leaves, cinnamon, and allspice; stir well. Dilute tomato paste in the water and add to dutch oven with wine. Bring to a boil, reduce heat to very low, cover, and simmer gently until meat is tender (2 to 2½ hours). Add water as needed to keep meat immersed in liquid at all times. Pan juices should be very thick when meat is done.

About 40 minutes before meat is done, heat oil in a large skillet over medium-high heat. Add onions and cook until golden brown on all sides (about 10 minutes). With a slotted utensil remove to paper towels to drain briefly. Add onions to dutch oven and simmer until meat is done.

Transfer stew to a large bowl to serve.

Serves 8

Meat Roll Stuffed with Eggs

Rolo

You may have trouble forming this meat roll the first time you make it, but it will become easier with practice. The aluminum foil is a great help in keeping the sheet of meat from cracking as you roll. Serve the meat roll with a side dish of tender-crisp green beans tossed in vinaigrette.

3 pounds lean ground beef
2 teaspoons minced fresh oregano or
  ½ teaspoon dried oregano, crushed
2 teaspoons minced fresh thyme or
  ½ teaspoon dried thyme, crushed
2 raw eggs, plus 6 hard-cooked eggs
1 clove garlic, finely minced
2 onions, finely minced
1½ cups fine dried bread crumbs
2 tablespoons chopped fresh parsley
¼ cup dry white wine
Salt and freshly ground pepper, to taste
Flour, for dusting
1 cup Basic Tomato Sauce (see page 178)
12 to 18 very small new potatoes, peeled

Preheat oven to 450° F. In a large mixing bowl, combine beef, oregano, thyme, raw eggs, garlic, onions, bread crumbs, parsley, wine, salt, and pepper. Mix well.

Dust a 12- by 18-inch piece of aluminum foil with flour. Press meat mixture on foil to cover foil evenly and completely. Arrange hard-cooked eggs, end to end, in a lengthwise line down center of meat. Lifting foil, carefully bring up one side of meat to cover eggs. Now roll meat around eggs to encase eggs completely, being careful not to trap foil inside seam of roll. With your hands shape roll so that it is a perfect cylinder; carefully remove foil and pat down meat to seal off ends of roll.

Place meat roll in a baking pan and bake for 20 minutes. Remove from oven and spoon tomato sauce over roll. Reduce oven temperature to 350° F. Return meat roll to oven and bake until cooked through (about 45 minutes).

While roll is cooking bring a large pot filled with water to a boil. Parboil potatoes 15 minutes; drain. Add potatoes to baking pan during last 20 minutes of cooking time; baste them with pan juices.

Transfer roll to a heated platter. Arrange potatoes around roll. Pour pan juices into a bowl, to be spooned over potatoes. Cut roll in 1- to 2-inch slices to serve.

Serves 6 to 8

Boiled Beef with Vegetables

Vothino Vrasto

*H*ere is a two-course meal cooked in one pot—a flavorful broth with pasta for the first course, followed by tender boiled beef and assorted vegetables. Look for the *fides* (fine noodles) or *kritharaki* (rice-shaped pasta) in a Greek market or specialty food shop. Garlic Sauce (see page 176) is a good condiment for the beef. Round out the menu with Beet and Onion Salad (see page 45), a loaf of crusty bread, and red wine.

1 beef chuck roast (3 to 4 lb)
2 to 3 pounds beef bones with marrow,
    sawed in 2-inch lengths
3 onions, halved
2 bay leaves
2 cloves garlic
2 stalks celery
6 to 8 leeks (white part only)
6 to 8 small carrots, scraped
6 to 8 small new potatoes, peeled
1 can (28 oz) plum tomatoes, chopped,
    with their liquid
Salt and freshly ground pepper, to taste
¼ pound fides, kritharaki, or coiled
    vermicelli

Place roast and bones in a large, heavy-bottomed pot. Add water to cover and bring to a boil. Skim off any foam that forms on the surface. Add onions, bay leaves, garlic, and celery. Cover, reduce heat, and simmer until meat is very tender (2 to 2½ hours). Add water as needed to keep beef completely immersed.

About 30 minutes before meat is done, add leeks, carrots, and potatoes to pot; cook until tender. Remove meat, leeks, carrots, potatoes, and bones to a platter; keep warm in a low oven.

Strain broth and return liquid to pot. Ladle off and discard any fat on the surface. Add tomatoes and bring to a boil. Season with salt and pepper. Add pasta and cook until tender.

Serve pasta in broth in shallow bowls as a first course. Slice the meat and arrange on a platter with the leeks, carrots, and potatoes for the second course. Pass the bones to those guests who wish to scoop out the buttery marrow.

Serves 6 to 8 as a first and second course

Meatballs with Mint
Keftaides

GGGGGGGGGGGGGGGGGGGGGGGGGGGGGGGGGGGGGGGGGGGGGGGGGGGGGGGGGGGGGGGGGGGG

Although these meatballs are traditionally formed into large spheres, I prefer to shape the mixture into patties. Serve with Athenian Macaroni (see page 71) and boiled dandelion greens for a real home-style meal.

> 1 pound each lean ground beef and veal
>   or pork
> 2 eggs
> 1 large onion, grated
> 1 tablespoon each minced fresh mint
>   and oregano
> 2 tablespoons minced fresh parsley
> 2 cloves garlic, minced
> 1 tablespoon tomato paste diluted in
>   1 tablespoon water
> 2 tablespoons olive oil, plus olive oil for
>   panfrying
> About 12 salted wheat crackers, soaked
>   in water and squeezed dry
> ½ cup dry white wine
> Salt and freshly ground pepper, to taste
> Flour, for dusting

Place meat in a large mixing bowl. Break in eggs and mix well. Add onion, mint, oregano, parsley, garlic, diluted tomato paste, the 2 tablespoons oil, crackers, wine, salt, and pepper. Knead until well mixed and smooth.

On a lightly floured board, shape meat mixture into 12 balls. With your palms, flatten balls into patties, then dust patties lightly with flour.

In a large skillet over medium heat, warm the remaining oil. Fry patties, turning once, until browned on both sides, 2 to 3 minutes per side or until done to your liking. Remove to heated platter and serve immediately.

Serves 6

Meatballs With Eggs and Tomato Sauce (Keftaides me Saltsa Domata) Preheat oven to 350° F. Prepare and fry patties as directed and arrange in a shallow baking dish. Pour 1½ cups Quick Tomato Sauce (see page 177) over patties. Lightly beat 8 eggs and pour evenly over top. Bake until egg mixture is set (about 30 minutes). Cut in squares to serve.

Meat Sausages in Wine Sauce
Souzoukakia

This is an old-fashioned dish that is rapidly disappearing from the Greek-American table. The sausages must be very finely textured, a consistency that can be achieved only by vigorous kneading of the meat.

Cinnamon-Tomato Sauce (see following recipe)
1 pound each finely ground beef and veal
2 eggs
2 cloves garlic, minced
3 tablespoons chopped fresh parsley
1 tablespoon tomato paste
Salt and freshly ground pepper, to taste
Flour, for coating
¼ cup butter
1 cup dry white wine

Prepare sauce and reserve in skillet. Place meat in a large mixing bowl. Break in eggs and mix well. Add garlic, parsley, tomato paste, salt, and pepper. Knead until well mixed and very smooth.

Form meat mixture into slender sausage shapes, making each about 3 inches long. Lightly roll sausages in flour.

In a large skillet over medium-high heat, melt butter. Add sausages and brown lightly on all sides. Add wine and just enough water to cover sausages. Transfer sausages and pan juices to skillet holding sauce.

Cover and simmer over low heat until sausages are cooked (20 to 30 minutes).

Serves 6

Cinnamon-Tomato Sauce

¾ cup tomato paste
1 cup water
1 clove garlic, minced
Dash ground cinnamon
1 teaspoon sugar
Salt and freshly ground pepper, to taste

In a large skillet over medium heat, combine tomato paste and the water; stir to blend. Add remaining ingredients and mix well. Reduce heat and simmer 20 minutes.

Calves' Liver with Oregano
Sikotaki Riganato

𝐺𝐺𝐺𝐺𝐺𝐺𝐺𝐺𝐺𝐺𝐺𝐺𝐺𝐺𝐺𝐺𝐺𝐺𝐺𝐺𝐺𝐺𝐺𝐺𝐺𝐺𝐺𝐺𝐺𝐺𝐺

The Greek pantry staples—oregano, olive oil, lemons—appear here with tender young liver. Cook the liver briefly over fairly high heat. It should be a rosy pink in the center when served. Accompany the liver with Rice and Fides Pilaf (see page 66), sliced tomatoes topped with feta cheese, and fresh bread for soaking up the sauce.

Flour, for dredging
Salt and freshly ground pepper, to taste
2 pounds calves' liver, trimmed and cut
*   in 6 serving pieces*
2 tablespoons butter
3 tablespoons olive oil
Minced fresh oregano, to taste
Juice of 1 or 2 lemons

Place flour in a wide, shallow bowl and season with salt and pepper. Dredge liver pieces in flour.

In a large skillet over high meat, melt butter with 1 tablespoon of the oil. Add liver pieces and fry on both sides, turning once, until golden (about 5 minutes total cooking time). Top each piece with a sprinkling of oregano and a squeeze of lemon juice.

Add remaining oil to skillet and heat briefly; rapidly move pan back and forth over burner just enough to mix ingredients. Cover pan, remove from heat, and let stand a few minutes.

Transfer liver to a heated platter and pour pan juices over the top. Serve immediately.

Serves 6

Tripe Sauté
Skembe me Salt

𝐺𝐺𝐺𝐺𝐺𝐺𝐺𝐺𝐺𝐺𝐺𝐺𝐺𝐺𝐺𝐺𝐺𝐺𝐺𝐺𝐺𝐺𝐺𝐺𝐺𝐺𝐺𝐺𝐺𝐺𝐺𝐺𝐺𝐺𝐺

Serve the tripe over a mound of Rice Pilaf (see page 67) with a bottle of full-bodied red wine.

2 pounds tripe
2 onions, 1 quartered, 1 thinly sliced
2 cloves garlic, 1 halved, 1 minced
4 bay leaves
Butter, for sautéing
Pinch dried oregano, crushed
4 ripe tomatoes, peeled and diced
½ cup dry white wine
Salt and freshly ground pepper, to taste

Rinse tripe with cold water, drain well, and place in a saucepan. Add quartered onion and halved garlic clove to saucepan. Add 2 of the bay leaves and pour in water to cover; bring to a boil. Reduce heat to low, cover, and simmer until tender (about 2 hours).

When tripe is almost done, melt butter in a large skillet over medium heat; add sliced onion and sauté until translucent (about 5 minutes). Add minced garlic, oregano, tomatoes, wine, salt, pepper, and the 2 remaining bay leaves. Stir well and simmer 5 minutes.

Drain tripe and cut in ¾-inch-wide strips. Add to skillet and simmer, covered, over low heat until flavors are well blended (30 to 45 minutes). Add a little water to pan if needed to cover tripe.

Transfer to a deep bowl to serve.

Serves 6

Roast Sucking Pig
Gourounopoulo Psito

Although roast suckling pig is not as coveted by the Greeks as roast lamb or kid, it is nonetheless considered a very special meal and is often served at Christmas. Have a butcher dress the suckling pig for roasting; be sure to ask for the heart and liver, which are used in the stuffing. The preferred roasting method is on a spit over hot charcoal, but here is a simpler method that can be done in the oven. Greeks are very fond of roasted potatoes and often, even if there is a stuffing, will surround the roasting pig with small new potatoes, bathing them in the pan juices until they turn chestnut brown. Accompany this dish with Apples Stuffed With Raisins and Nuts (see page 54).

Fruit and Herb Stuffing (see following recipe)
1 suckling pig (10 to 12 lb) dressed
Salt, freshly ground pepper, and minced fresh oregano, to taste
½ cup butter, melted and cooled
Juice of 2 lemons
1 red apple
Raisins or cherries
Parsley and/or watercress sprigs, for garnish

Wash pig inside and out with cold water; dry thoroughly. Rub cavity with salt, pepper, and oregano. Pack stuffing into cavity and skewer closed, securing with twine.

Place a ball of aluminum foil or a block of wood in the pig's mouth, to be replaced later by the traditional apple. Pull front legs of pig forward so they stretch straight beyond head; bind together with wire or string. Pull hind legs straight back and secure them together. Cover the pig's ears with foil to prevent burning.

Preheat oven to 375°. In a small bowl mix together butter and lemon juice and rub mixture over entire surface of pig. Place pig in a roasting pan and cover pig with aluminum foil. If desired, insert a meat thermometer in thickest part of pig. Roast about 30 minutes per pound, basting often with pan juices. Remove foil the last 30 minutes of cooking time. The thermometer should register an internal temperature of about 160° F when pig is done.

Remove pig from oven and place on wooden board. Replace mouth wedge with apple and mark eyes with raisins. Remove foil from ears and unbind legs. Transfer to a large serving platter and garnish with parsley. Carve at the table.

Serves 6 to 8

Fruit and Herb Stuffing

1 cup dried currants
1 cup dry white wine
2 tablespoons butter
1 pound lean ground pork
Liver and heart of pig, chopped
1 cup finely chopped celery
3 tablespoons chopped fresh parsley
2 cloves garlic, minced
1 cup cooked long-grain white rice
2 cups grated apple

Continued—

*2 pounds small white onions (about
    1 inch in diameter)*
*2 teaspoons minced fresh thyme or
    ½ teaspoon dried thyme, crushed*
*2 teaspoons minced fresh rosemary or
    ½ teaspoon dried rosemary, crushed*
2 eggs, lightly beaten
Salt and freshly ground pepper, to taste

In a small bowl combine currants and wine; set aside.

In a large skillet over medium heat, melt butter. Add pork, liver, and heart and sauté a few minutes. Stir in celery, parsley, and garlic; sauté 5 minutes. Add rice, apple, onions, thyme, rosemary, eggs, and currants and wine. Stir briefly and remove from heat. Season with salt and pepper. Cool before stuffing pig.

Pork and Celery with Egg-Lemon Sauce
Hirino me Selino Avgolemono

The ancient Greeks used celery, a native of the eastern Mediterranean, as a seasoning only. Modern Greeks, however, have elevated celery's status to that of a full-fledged vegetable.

¼ cup butter
*3 pounds lean boneless pork, cut in 1- to
    1½-inch cubes*
2 onions, chopped
1 clove garlic, minced
2 tablespoons flour
3 tablespoons water
2 tablespoons chopped fresh parsley
Salt and freshly ground pepper, to taste
½ cup dry white wine
4 celery hearts
*Egg-Lemon Sauce (see page 173), made
    with pan juices*

In a deep skillet over medium heat, melt butter. Add pork, onions, and garlic. Sauté until lightly browned (about 7 minutes). Dissolve flour in the water and add to skillet with parsley, salt, and pepper; stir well. Add wine and just enough water to cover meat. Cover and simmer over low heat until pork is tender (about 1 hour).

While pork is cooking, trim celery hearts and cut in half lengthwise. About 20 minutes before pork is done, add celery hearts to pan, spooning pan juices over them. Simmer until celery hearts are tender; do not overcook. Remove skillet from heat.

Prepare Egg-Lemon Sauce, using pan juices for the liquid. Return contents of skillet to serving temperature. Add sauce to skillet and stir well; do not boil. Remove from heat, cover, and let stand a few minutes before serving.

Serves 8

Artemis, the Goddess of the Hunt

Hers is a pageant in savagery.
Her statuesque boylike figure
draped in a short tunic,
revealing the strength of her legs.
Her reign over wildlife
is resplendent in folklore.
Her deeds are terrible in vengeance,
yet infinitely tender to wildlife.
So goes the tale of our virgin huntress,
who asked nothing more than
to roam the mountain without artifice,
save only a hunter's garb.
Today she stands in the Louvre,
there for posterity,
the fearless and superb figure of Artemis,
a maternal hand upon the deer. . . .
I wonder, dare I encounter her wrath
as I prepare game?

ARTEMIS AND THE FOODS FROM THE HUNT

In the rolling hills of the Greek countryside, hunters still pursue game birds as they did in ancient times. The highly prized partridge and pheasant are stuffed with grains and roasted. Smaller game birds are often slipped onto spits and held over hot coals until they turn a deep bronze.

Autumn draws hunters into the mountain passes in search of deer. They come to look for rabbits, too, and then take them home and cook them in a richly spiced tomato sauce that infuses the meat with the fragrance of cinnamon and allspice.

More than twenty-five hundred years ago, Greeks had domesticated various fowl. They fattened geese, a great favorite, on grain to the point of obesity. Today geese are still served for special occasions, most often with their cavities stuffed with nuts and fruits. Duck, chicken, and even the New World turkey are popular, too, and the preparations for these birds are varied and delicious.

Game Birds, Rabbit, and Venison

*I*n Greece the *perdika,* ("partridge") and the *kickle* ("thrush") are the most popular of all wild birds for the table. Both have been hunted since ancient times.

Today partridges and other wild fowl are raised on farms in North America, but on a very small scale. Farm-raised pheasant, rabbit, and venison, however, are widely sold in better meat markets. All of the following recipes are worth the effort necessary to find a source for commercial game.

Roast Game Birds with Wild Rice Stuffing

Kotopoulo Kyniyo Yemisto

I have called for Rock Cornish game hens in this recipe, although partridge would be the best choice. The stuffing is made with wild rice, which gives a domestic bird a pleasantly gamey flavor. Serve this dish with pan drippings or Grape Sauce (see page 175), a mixed salad with Feta Dressing Evoula (see page 180), and a lightly chilled rosé. Use the birds' giblets for the stuffing.

Wild Rice Stuffing (see following recipe)
4 Rock Cornish game hens (about 1 lb each)
Salt and freshly ground pepper, to taste
Butter, for rubbing on birds
½ cup each dry white wine and water

Prepare stuffing. Preheat oven to 350° F.

Wash hens inside and out; dry thoroughly. Fill cavities with stuffing, packing firmly; secure openings closed with skewers. Sprinkle birds with salt and pepper and rub generously with butter. Place birds in a roasting pan. Drizzle wine over each bird and pour the water into pan.

Roast birds, basting frequently with pan juices, until browned and tender (about 45 minutes). Remove skewers before serving.

Wild Rice Stuffing

4 cups chicken stock
½ teaspoon salt
4 tablespoons butter
1 cup wild rice
Giblets from game hens, chopped
3 green onions, minced
¼ cup minced celery
2 cloves garlic, minced
2 tablespoons chopped fresh parsley
¼ teaspoon each dried thyme and sage, crushed
¼ cup pine nuts
¼ cup dry white wine

In a saucepan over high heat, bring stock to a boil. Add salt, 3 tablespoons of the butter, and wild rice; stir well. Cover, reduce heat to low, and cook until rice is tender and liquid is absorbed (30 to 40 minutes).

Meanwhile, melt the remaining butter in a large skillet over medium heat. Add giblets, onions, celery, garlic, parsley, thyme, and sage; sauté until onions and giblets are lightly browned (about 8 minutes). Stir in cooked rice and pine nuts. Add wine, stir well, and reduce heat. Cover and simmer 5 minutes. Cool before stuffing birds.

Serves 4

Pheasant Stuffed with Grapes

Fasianos Yemistos

*P*heasant is now being raised commercially in many regions of North America, so you won't need to rely on the kindness of a hunter to make this dish. The stuffing is truly a Greek-American creation, combining the wild rice native to the Midwest with traditional Mediterranean ingredients.

Grape Stuffing and Fruit Cup (see
*   following recipe)*
1 pheasant (about 3 lb)
½ cup plus 2 tablespoons butter, plus
*   butter for casserole*
1 clove garlic, minced
¼ cup vermouth
Salt and freshly ground pepper, to taste

Prepare stuffing and fruit cup. Preheat oven to 450° F.

Wash pheasant inside and out; dry thoroughly. In a large skillet over medium heat, melt the ½ cup butter. Add garlic and sauté briefly. Add pheasant and gently brown on all sides, basting constantly with butter. When evenly browned, remove pheasant to work surface; strain and reserve pan juices.

Fill pheasant cavity with stuffing; secure opening closed with skewers and truss legs with kitchen twine. Place any remaining stuffing in a covered casserole to be baked along with pheasant.

Butter a large earthenware casserole or a dutch oven. Line with a sheet of aluminum foil large enough to enclose bird completely. Place pheasant in center of foil; pour reserved pan juices over top, then drizzle with vermouth. Sprinkle lightly with salt and pepper and rub the remaining 2 tablespoons butter over skin. Fold foil over bird and seal securely.

Cover casserole and roast 25 minutes. Remove from oven and unfold foil; baste bird with pan juices and refold foil securely. Return to oven and roast 1 hour. Remove from oven, unfold foil to expose bird, and baste with pan juices. Return to oven, uncovered; roast 20 minutes more, basting occasionally.

Remove pheasant and casserole of stuffing from oven; transfer bird to a heated platter. Pour pheasant pan juices into a small skillet; skim off and discard fat. Heat to serving temperature, season with salt and pepper, and pour into a serving bowl.

Remove twine and skewers from pheasant; scoop out stuffing into a serving bowl before carving bird. Accompany carved pheasant with pan juices, fruit cup, and stuffing.

Serves 4

Grape Stuffing and Fruit Cup

4 cups chicken stock
1 cup wild rice
Salt, to taste
2 or 3 small seedless oranges
½ cup butter
Pheasant giblets, finely chopped
4 green onions, minced
2 stalks celery, minced
1 teaspoon chopped fresh parsley
1 cup small seedless grapes
½ cup vermouth
Freshly ground pepper, to taste
1 cup plain yogurt

In a saucepan over high heat, bring stock to a boil. Add rice and salt, stir well, and cover. Reduce heat to low and cook until rice is tender and liquid is absorbed (30 to 40 minutes).

Peel oranges and remove all of the white membrane. Divide into sections, discarding white pith and strings. Set aside.

In a large skillet over medium heat, melt ¼ cup of the butter. Add giblets, onions, celery, and parsley; sauté over low heat until giblets are lightly browned (about 10 minutes). Add cooked rice and toss to mix. Gently mix in half of the grapes, half of the orange sections, the remaining butter, and vermouth. Cook 5 minutes and remove from heat. Cool before stuffing bird.

To prepare fruit cup, in a medium bowl combine remaining grapes and orange pieces with yogurt. Cover and chill well.

Rabbit in Foil
Lagos Kleftiko

*T*his is a contribution from my father's vast repertoire of recipes. The onions, tomato, and seasonings in the dish are those of the classic Greek *stefado* (stew) preparation, but the rabbit is wrapped in foil, *kleftiko* ("bandit") style, to preserve its delicate flavor. My father liked to serve the rabbit with small new potatoes, first parboiled and then browned in the oven. The savory sauce is delicious spooned over the potatoes. Complete the menu with crusty bread and a green salad.

1 rabbit (2½ to 3 lb), dressed
1 cup wine vinegar
2 whole cloves
1 onion, sliced
2 bay leaves
2 cinnamon sticks (each about
*   2 in. long)*
3 cloves garlic, minced
1 teaspoon ground allspice
Salt and freshly ground pepper, to taste
6 tablespoons olive oil, plus olive oil for
*   roasting pan*
16 small (about 1 inch in diameter)
*   white onions, peeled*
1 cup Basic Tomato Sauce (see page 178)

Cut rabbit in serving pieces and place in a ceramic or glass bowl. Add vinegar, cloves, onion, bay leaves, cinnamon, garlic, allspice, salt, and pepper; turn rabbit pieces in marinade to coat thoroughly. Cover and refrigerate overnight, turning pieces occasionally.

Preheat oven to 350° F. Lift rabbit pieces from marinade and reserve marinade. In a large skillet over medium heat, warm 3 tablespoons of the oil. Brown rabbit on all sides, then remove to paper towels to drain.

In the same skillet over medium heat, warm the remaining 3 tablespoons oil. Add onions and sauté until golden brown on all sides (about 10 minutes). Set aside.

Ready a long, double-thick sheet of aluminum foil large enough to enclose the rabbit pieces. Arrange rabbit pieces in a row down center of foil, then bring sides and ends of foil up to form a boat shape. Combine reserved marinade with tomato sauce and spoon over rabbit. Then spoon reserved onions over and around rabbit.

Fold foil over rabbit and seal securely. Oil a roasting pan and place rabbit in it. Roast until rabbit is tender (about 1½ hours).

Transfer rabbit in foil to a serving platter and unwrap at table.

Serves 4

Venison Steaks with Tomato Sauce
Elafi me Saltsa Domata

$\mathcal{M}$arinate the venison overnight, so that the meat will be infused with the flavors of the seasonings. Cook the steaks quickly, removing them from the broiler while they are still rosy in the center. Serve with Potatoes Browned in Butter (see page 60) and a dry white wine.

1 cup dry white wine
½ cup olive oil
1 bay leaf, crushed
2 cloves garlic, crushed
½ cup white wine vinegar
Pinch each ground cloves and dried
    thyme, crushed
6 venison steaks
Fresh Tomato Sauce (see following
    recipe)
Melted butter, for brushing steaks

In a ceramic or glass bowl, combine wine, oil, bay leaf, garlic, vinegar, cloves, and thyme. Add steaks and turn to coat evenly. Cover and refrigerate at least 2 hours, but preferably overnight; turn steaks occasionally.

Preheat broiler. Remove steaks from marinade; strain marinade and reserve. Set steaks aside. Prepare tomato sauce; keep warm.

Brush steaks with melted butter and place on a rack on a broiler pan. Slip under broiler and cook on both sides, turning once, until done to taste. Timing will depend upon thickness of steaks; for a 1-inch-thick steak, plan on about 4 minutes on each side for medium-rare.

Remove steaks to a heated platter and pour hot tomato sauce over top. Serve immediately.

Serves 6

Fresh Tomato Sauce

½ cup butter
1 onion, minced
1 clove garlic, minced
4 ripe tomatoes, peeled and chopped
1 cup white wine
Reserved strained marinade from
    venison steaks
Salt and freshly ground pepper, to taste

In a skillet over medium-high heat, melt butter. Add onion and garlic and sauté until translucent (about 5 minutes).

Add tomatoes and cook 5 minutes. Add wine, reserved marinade, salt, and pepper. Stir well and simmer, uncovered, 25 minutes.

🔸🔸

The Greek penchant for stuffing fowl carries over to domesticated birds, as illustrated in the following array of recipes for turkey, goose, duck and squab. When it comes to chicken, however, no generalization applies. Greeks love it stuffed and roasted, braised with vegetables on the stove-top, or simmered in a yogurt sauce.

Roast Turkey with Chestnut Stuffing
Galopoulo Yemisto

🔸🔸

This turkey is stuffed with an elaborate marriage of nuts, meats, and spices. The result is a meal to tempt the mortals. The gods will already be on your side. Note that you need the turkey giblets for the stuffing.

Chestnut Stuffing (see following recipe)
1 turkey (12 to 14 lb)
Salt and freshly ground pepper, to taste
Butter, for rubbing on turkey
2 cloves garlic, crushed (optional)
Olive oil, for cheesecloth
Melted butter mixed with freshly
  squeezed lemon juice to taste, for
  basting
Dry white wine and brandy, to taste

Prepare stuffing. Preheat oven to 300° F.

Wash turkey inside and out; dry thoroughly. Sprinkle cavity with salt and pepper. Fill cavity with stuffing; secure opening closed with skewers and truss legs with kitchen twine. Liberally rub turkey skin with butter and garlic (if used). Season skin with salt and pepper.

Place turkey in a roasting pan. Dampen a piece of cheesecloth with oil and drape over the breast. Roast 20 minutes per pound (4 hours to 4 hours and 40 minutes, depending on size of bird), basting often with butter-lemon mixture. Thirty minutes before bird is ready, remove cheesecloth. Sprinkle turkey lightly with wine and brandy and roast until golden.

When turkey is done, remove from rack to a wooden board or large platter. Cover loosely with foil and let rest about 20 minutes. Remove twine and skewers; scoop out stuffing into a serving bowl before carving.

Serves 12 to 15

Chestnut Stuffing

1 pound chestnuts
¼ cup dried currants
2 cups dry white wine
¼ cup butter
1 pound lean ground beef
Turkey giblets, finely chopped
1 clove garlic, minced
2 onions, finely chopped
1 cup finely chopped celery
½ cup minced fresh parsley
1 tablespoon poultry seasoning
1 teaspoon each ground cinnamon and
*   dried fines herbes, crushed*
1 cup long-grain white rice
½ cup each pine nuts and chopped
*   walnuts*
1 cup Basic Tomato Sauce (see page 178)
Salt and freshly ground pepper, to taste

Preheat oven to 350° F. With a sharp knife cut an *X* on the flat side of each chestnut. Place on a baking sheet and roast 10 minutes. When chestnuts are cool enough to handle, peel off tough outer shell and brown fuzzy membrane. Place in a saucepan with water to cover and bring to a boil. Reduce heat and simmer about 15 minutes. Drain, cool, and chop; set aside.

In a small bowl combine currants and 1 cup of the wine; set aside.

In a large skillet over medium-high heat, melt butter. Add beef, giblets, and garlic; sauté 5 minutes. Add onions, celery, parsley, poultry seasoning, cinnamon, and fines herbes; sauté until onions are translucent and ingredients are well mixed (about 5 minutes).

Add rice, reserved chestnuts, pine nuts, walnuts, tomato sauce, and currant-wine mixture. Mix well and simmer over low heat 20 minutes. Season with salt and pepper and mix in the remaining wine. Stir well and remove from heat. Cool before stuffing bird.

Roast Goose with Chestnut-Apple Stuffing

Chena Yemiste

The dark, luxurious meat of the goose will surely convert even dedicated white-meat lovers. The bird is very high in fat, however, so remove as much fat as possible from the cavity before adding the stuffing. Accompany this extraordinary bird with the regal accompaniments it deserves. Start with Chilled Chicken and Egg-Lemon Soup (see page 33) and complete your feast with Orange-Almond Crêpes (see page 78). Note that you need the goose giblets to make the stuffing.

Chestnut-Apple Stuffing (see following recipe)
1 goose (10 to 12 lb)
Salt and freshly ground pepper, to taste
Orange-flavored liqueur, to taste
Parsley sprigs and orange slices, for garnish

Prepare stuffing. Preheat oven to 325° F.

Wash goose inside and out; dry thoroughly. Sprinkle cavity with salt and pepper. Fill cavity with stuffing; secure opening closed with skewers and truss legs with kitchen twine. Place goose, breast side up, in roasting pan. With the tip of a knife, pierce skin in several places so fat can drain off during roasting.

Roast until done to taste (about 3½ hours). During roasting, occasionally skim fat from pan juices with a bulb baster. About 10 minutes before goose is ready, remove all fat from pan with bulb baster, then generously sprinkle goose with liqueur.

When goose is done, transfer to a wooden board or platter, cover loosely with foil, and let rest 15 minutes. Pour pan juices into a small pan and heat to serving temperature; adjust seasoning with salt and pepper. Pour into a serving bowl.

Remove twine and skewers from goose; scoop out stuffing into a serving bowl. Carve bird and arrange on heated platter. Garnish with parsley and orange slices. Serve sliced goose with stuffing and pan juices alongside.

Serves 6 to 8

Chestnut-Apple Stuffing

½ cup raisins
¼ cup orange-flavored liqueur
1 pound chestnuts
2 cups chicken stock
½ cup wild rice
½ cup butter
Giblets from goose, finely chopped
1 cup chopped onion
1 cup chopped celery
1 clove garlic, minced
½ cup chopped fresh parsley
2 cups grated apple
1 cup slivered blanched almonds
1 cup dry white wine
1 teaspoon poultry seasoning
½ teaspoon ground cinnamon
Salt and freshly ground pepper, to taste

Continued—

Preheat oven to 350° F. In a small bowl combine raisins and liqueur; set aside.

With a sharp knife cut an *X* on the flat side of each chestnut. Place on a baking sheet and roast 10 minutes. When chestnuts are cool enough to handle, peel off tough outer shell and brown fuzzy membrane. Place in a saucepan with water to cover and bring to a boil. Reduce heat and simmer about 15 minutes. Drain, cool, and chop; set aside.

Meanwhile, in a saucepan bring stock to a boil. Add rice, stir well, and cover. Reduce heat to low and cook until rice is tender and liquid is absorbed (30 to 40 minutes).

In a large skillet over medium heat, melt butter. Add giblets, onions, celery, garlic, and parsley; sauté until mixture is lightly browned (about 8 minutes). Add cooked rice and reserved chestnuts and toss to combine. Mix in apple, almonds, wine, and raisin-liqueur mixture. Cook briefly. Season with poultry seasoning, cinnamon, salt, and pepper. Remove from heat and cool before stuffing bird.

Roast Duck in Wine with Potatoes
Papaki Psito me Patates

*A*ccompany this home-style dish with greens tossed with vinaigrette, and for dessert a carafe of red wine and fruit and cheese.

1 duck (about 4½ lb), with giblets
Salt and freshly ground pepper, to taste
1 clove garlic, minced
Freshly squeezed lemon juice, to taste
¼ cup butter
1 cup chicken stock
1 cup plus 3 tablespoons dry sherry
1 bay leaf
12 small new potatoes, peeled
4 ripe tomatoes, peeled and chopped
Minced fresh oregano, to taste

Preheat oven to 350° F. Finely chop giblets and set aside.

Cut duck in quarters and trim off as much fat as possible. Rub duck quarters with salt, pepper, garlic, and lemon juice. In a roasting pan placed on stove-top, melt butter. Add duck pieces and brown on all sides. Pour off and discard fat.

Add stock, the 1 cup sherry, bay leaf, and reserved giblets to duck pieces in roasting pan. Bake 40 minutes.

Meanwhile, place potatoes in a saucepan with water to cover and bring to a boil. Parboil 15 minutes; drain.

Add potatoes and tomatoes to roasting pan; sprinkle the 3 tablespoons sherry and the oregano over duck and vegetables. Cook until duck is tender (30 to 45 minutes).

To serve, transfer duck and vegetables to a heated shallow serving dish.

Serves 4

Roast Duck with Apple Stuffing

Papaki Yemisto

Greek mythology contains many references to apples. Zeus and Hera were given apples as a wedding present, and golden apples were dropped in the path of the fleet-footed Atalanta, causing her to lose a coveted footrace. Although the apples of the distant past would probably bear little resemblance to the crunchy varieties of today, Zeus and his companions would certainly relish this apple-rich stuffing. Note that you need the ducks' giblets for the stuffing.

Apple Stuffing (see following recipe)
2 ducks (about 4½ lb each)
Salt and freshly ground pepper, to taste
2 tablespoons butter, softened
2 cloves garlic, crushed
Melted butter mixed with freshly
*   squeezed lemon juice to taste, for*
*   basting*
Orange-flavored liqueur, to taste
Parsley sprigs and orange slices, for
*   garnish*

Prepare stuffing. Preheat oven to 350° F.

Wash ducks inside and out; dry thoroughly. Rub cavities with salt and pepper. Loosely fill each cavity with stuffing; secure openings closed with skewers and truss legs with kitchen twine. Place remaining stuffing in a covered casserole to cook along with duck. Sprinkle ducks with salt and pepper. Combine softened butter with garlic and rub on ducks. Place ducks in a large roasting pan. With the tip of a knife, prick skin of ducks in several places so fat can drain off during cooking.

Roast ducks, basting occasionally with butter-lemon mixture and skimming fat from pan juices with a bulb baster.

After about 1¼ hours increase oven temperature to 450° F. Remove all fat from pan juices with bulb baster, then generously sprinkle ducks with liqueur. Roast, basting frequently with pan juices, until meat is tender and skin is crisp (about 20 minutes).

When ducks are done to taste, transfer to a wooden board or platter, cover loosely with aluminum foil, and let rest about 10 minutes. Pour pan juices into a small pan and heat to serving temperature; adjust seasoning. Pour into a serving bowl.

Remove twine and skewers from ducks; scoop out stuffing into a serving bowl. Cut ducks in serving pieces and arrange on a heated platter. Garnish with beds of parsley topped with orange slices. Serve stuffing and pan juices alongside.

Serves 8

Apple Stuffing

2 quarts chicken stock
2 cups wild rice
3 cups grated tart apple
1 cup dry sherry
6 tablespoons butter
Giblets from ducks, finely chopped
1 cup chopped celery
½ cup chopped green onion
1 clove garlic, minced
1 cup pine nuts
2 teaspoons freshly grated orange zest
2 tablespoons orange-flavored liqueur
Salt and freshly ground pepper, to taste

In a saucepan over high heat, bring stock to a boil. Add rice, stir well, and cover. Reduce heat to low and cook until rice is tender and liquid is absorbed (30 to 40 minutes).

In a medium bowl combine apple and sherry; set aside. In a large skillet over medium heat, melt 4 tablespoons of the butter. Add giblets, celery, onion, and garlic; sauté until mixture is lightly browned (about 10 minutes). Add cooked rice, apple-sherry mixture, and pine nuts; toss to combine. Stir in orange zest, liqueur, and the remaining butter and heat briefly. Remove from heat and season with salt and pepper. Cool before stuffing bird.

Stuffed Squabs in Foil

Peristeri sto Harti

These domesticated pigeons have rich, dark meat that roasts beautifully. Although squabs can sometimes be found in the frozen meat section of supermarkets, it is best if you look for fresh birds. Asian poultry markets and specialty butchers will have them on hand or will be able to order them for you. Note that you need the birds' giblets to make the stuffing.

Raisin-Rice Stuffing (see following recipe)
4 squabs (about ¾ lb each)
¼ cup butter, plus melted butter for
*   basting*
Dried fines herbes, crushed
Brandy, for basting

Prepare stuffing. Preheat oven to 350° F.

Wash squabs inside and out; dry thoroughly. In a large skillet over medium heat, melt the ¼ cup butter. Add squabs and carefully brown on all sides. Remove to paper towels to drain; cool.

Fill each squab cavity with stuffing and secure closed with skewers. Put any remaining stuffing in a covered casserole to be cooked along with birds.

For each squab ready a double-thick sheet of aluminum foil large enough to enclose bird. Place a squab in center of each sheet and sprinkle with herbs. Baste with melted butter and brandy. Fold foil around squabs and seal securely.

Place squabs in a roasting pan. Roast until tender (about 40 minutes). Remove skewers before serving.

Serves 4

Raisin-Rice Stuffing

2 cups chicken stock
1 cup long-grain white rice
4 tablespoons butter
2 tablespoons minced celery
Squab giblets, finely chopped
½ teaspoon dried fines herbes, crushed
3 tablespoons golden raisins
¼ cup chopped walnuts
Dash brandy

In a saucepan over high heat, bring stock to a boil. Add rice and 1 tablespoon of the butter; stir well and cover. Reduce heat to low and cook until rice is tender and liquid is absorbed (about 20 minutes).

In a large skillet over medium heat, melt the remaining butter. Add celery and giblets and sauté until lightly browned (about 5 minutes). Add herbs and cooked rice and toss to combine. Mix in raisins, walnuts, and brandy; reduce heat and cook 5 to 10 minutes. Cool before stuffing birds.

Artichoke-Stuffed Chicken in Foil
Kota Yemista sto Harti

*F*rozen artichoke hearts shorten the preparation time for this dish. If you prefer fresh artichokes, use only the tender hearts and parboil as directed for the frozen hearts. Use the bird's giblets to prepare the stuffing.

Artichoke Stuffing (see following recipe)
1 roasting chicken (about 3½ lb)
Salt and freshly ground pepper, to taste
¼ cup butter, plus melted butter for
*   aluminum foil*
½ cup brandy

Prepare stuffing. Preheat oven to 350 F.

Wash chicken inside and out; dry thoroughly. Season cavity and skin with salt and pepper.

In a large, deep skillet or dutch oven, melt the ¼ cup butter. Brown chicken on all sides, turning carefully with 2 large spoons so that you do not prick the skin. Remove chicken to a work surface; strain butter and reserve.

Fill chicken cavity with stuffing; secure opening closed with skewers and truss legs with kitchen twine. Place remaining stuffing in a covered casserole to bake along with chicken.

Ready a double-thick sheet of aluminum foil large enough to enclose the chicken. Place chicken on foil and bring sides and ends up to form a boat shape. Pour strained butter over chicken, then drizzle with brandy. Fold foil over chicken and seal securely.

Place chicken in a roasting pan and cook until tender (about 1½ hours). Remove from oven, unwrap, and place on a platter. Cover loosely with foil and let rest 10 minutes.

Remove skewers and twine. Scoop out stuffing into a serving bowl. Carve chicken and serve.

Serves 3 or 4

Artichoke Stuffing

2 cups chicken stock
1 cup long-grain white rice
6 tablespoons butter
1 package (10 oz) frozen artichoke
*   hearts*
Giblets from chicken, finely chopped
1 tablespoon chopped fresh parsley
1 clove garlic, minced
2 green onions, chopped
Salt and freshly ground pepper, to taste

In a saucepan over high heat, bring stock to a boil. Add rice and 2 tablespoons of the butter; stir well. Cover, reduce heat to low, and cook until rice is tender and liquid is absorbed (about 20 minutes).

Meanwhile, bring a saucepan filled with water to a boil. Add artichoke hearts and parboil 8 minutes; drain and set aside.

In a large skillet over medium heat, melt the remaining butter. Add giblets, parsley, garlic, and onions; sauté until mixture is lightly browned (about 10 minutes). Add cooked rice and toss to combine. Add artichoke hearts and mix gently with rice. Season with salt and pepper. Cool before stuffing bird.

Roast Stuffed Chicken, Plaka Style
Kota Yemista à la Plaka

Serve this delectable Athenian-inspired chicken with a bowl of chilled Homemade Yogurt (see page 181); the yogurt will help balance the richness of the chicken. Complete the menu with Artichokes Fried in Olive Oil (see page 62), a chilled white retsina, and fruit and cheese for dessert. Note that you need the chickens' giblets to prepare the stuffing.

Rice and Nut Stuffing (see following recipe)
2 roasting chickens (about 3 lb each)
Salt and freshly ground pepper, to taste
1 cup each dry white wine and water
Melted butter, for basting
Lemon wedges, for garnish

Prepare stuffing. Preheat oven to 350° F.

Wash chickens inside and out; dry thoroughly. Sprinkle cavities with salt and pepper and fill with stuffing; secure openings closed with skewers and truss legs together with kitchen twine. Place chickens in a large roasting pan. Pour wine over chickens and pour the water into roasting pan.

Roast chickens, basting frequently with butter, until tender (about 1½ hours).

Remove chickens to a heated platter. Cover loosely with foil and let rest 10 minutes. Pour pan juices into a small pan and heat to serving temperature; adjust seasoning with salt and pepper. Pour into a serving bowl.

Remove skewers and twine from chickens; scoop out stuffing into a serving bowl. Cut chicken in serving pieces and arrange on platter; garnish with lemon wedges. Serve pan juices and stuffing alongside.

Rice and Nut Stuffing

3 tablespoons dried currants
½ cup dry white wine
2 cups chicken stock
1 cup long-grain white rice
6 tablespoons butter
Giblets from chickens, finely chopped
¼ pound chicken livers, finely chopped
1 medium onion, finely chopped
2 cloves garlic, minced
*2 tablespoons each chopped fresh parsley
   and celery*
¼ teaspoon poultry seasoning
½ cup pine nuts
2 tablespoons slivered blanched almonds
Salt and freshly ground pepper, to taste

In a small bowl combine currants and wine; set aside. In a saucepan over high heat, bring stock to a boil. Add rice, stir well, and cover. Reduce heat to low and cook until rice is tender and liquid is absorbed (about 20 minutes).

In a large skillet over medium heat, melt 4 tablespoons of the butter. Add giblets, livers, onion, garlic, parsley, and celery; sauté until mixture is lightly browned (about 10 minutes). Add poultry seasoning and mix well. Stir in currant-wine mixture, pine nuts, and almonds; cook over low heat 10 minutes. Add cooked rice and the remaining butter and toss to mix. Season with salt and pepper. Cool before stuffing bird.

Serves 6

Chicken Breasts with Pine-Nut Rice
Kota me Koukounari

██

*U*nkown to the ancient Greeks, the seeds of the stone pine (*Pinus pinea*) are used throughout the Mediterranean and the Middle East in sweet and savory dishes alike. Here they are combined with rice and chicken livers in a quick-to-assemble accompaniment for chicken breasts.

Pine-Nut Rice (see following recipe)
3 whole chicken breasts
Salt and freshly ground pepper, to taste
Butter, as needed
Dry white wine, to taste

Prepare rice. Preheat oven to 350° F.

Cut chicken breasts in half, then bone and skin. Season with salt and pepper. In a skillet over medium heat, melt butter. Add chicken breasts and sauté briefly until golden brown on both sides.

Place rice in bottom of a small baking dish. Arrange chicken breasts on top. Dot breasts with butter and sprinkle with a little wine. Bake until tender but still moist (about 30 minutes).

Pine Nut Rice

2 cups chicken stock
1 cup long-grain white rice
6 tablespoons butter
¼ pound chicken livers, chopped
2 tablespoons pine nuts
2 green onions, chopped
1 clove garlic, minced
3 tablespoons white wine
Salt and freshly ground pepper, to taste

In a saucepan over high heat, bring stock to a boil. Add rice and 2 tablespoons of the butter; stir well. Cover, reduce heat to low, and cook until rice is tender and liquid is absorbed (about 20 minutes).

In a skillet over medium-high heat, melt the remaining butter. Add livers, pine nuts, onions, and garlic; sauté until livers are just cooked and onions are translucent (about 5 minutes). Add wine and cooked rice and toss to combine. Season to taste with salt and pepper.

Serves 6

Sunday Chicken Dinner

Kota Avgolemono

This is a superb Sunday dinner, one my mother prepared often. A whole chicken is simmered with vegetables to yield the rich stock needed to make egg-lemon soup—the first course of this typical meal. Then the chicken is browned in the oven with potatoes. Round out the menu with Athenian Salad (see page 41) and feta cheese. Traditionally a stewing chicken is used, but this makes the recipe too time-consuming for those of us who also want to relax on Sunday. I prefer to cook a plump frying chicken.

1 frying chicken (3½ to 4 lb)
2 stalks celery
1 onion, quartered
Salt and freshly ground pepper, to taste
8 small new potatoes, peeled
2 cloves garlic, minced
Minced fresh oregano, to taste
2 tablespoons butter
Chicken and Egg-Lemon Soup
    (see page 33), made with stock from
    simmering chicken

Place chicken in a stockpot or dutch oven and add water to cover. Add celery, onion, salt, and pepper. Bring to a boil and skim off any foam that forms on surface. Reduce heat to low and simmer 45 minutes. Be careful not to pierce the skin of the chicken at any time as it simmers.

Meanwhile, preheat oven to 400° F. Fill a saucepan with water and bring to a boil. Add potatoes and parboil 15 minutes; drain.

Lift chicken from stock and place in a roasting pan. Strain stock and reserve for preparing avgolemono soup.

When chicken is cool enough to touch, rub garlic over skin. Add potatoes to roasting pan, arranging them around the chicken. Sprinkle chicken and potatoes with salt, pepper, and oregano. Dot chicken with butter. Pour 1 cup of the strained stock into the pan.

Roast chicken and potatoes, basting occasionally with pan juices, until golden brown (about 30 minutes).

While chicken is roasting, prepare soup, making it with the reserved strained stock. Serve soup as the first course; follow with the chicken and potatoes.

Serves 4

Chicken in Tomato Sauce with Macaroni

Kota Kapama

G G G G G G G G G G G G G G G G G G G G G G G G G G G G G G G G G G G G G G G G G G G G G G G G G G G G G G G G G G G G G G G G G G G G G G G G G G G G G G G G G G G G

A tossed green salad and fresh fruit for dessert complement this classic chicken dish served with buttery macaroni. Note that the chicken needs to marinate for two hours.

1 frying chicken (3½ to 4 lb), cut in
serving pieces
Juice of 1 lemon
Dash ground cinnamon
Salt and freshly ground pepper, to taste
2 cinnamon sticks (each about
2 in. long)
1 clove garlic, minced
3 or 4 tablespoons tomato paste
½ cup water
1 can (28 oz) plum tomatoes, coarsely
chopped, with their liquid
1 bay leaf
¼ cup olive oil
1 onion, sliced
½ cup dry sherry
Athenian Macaroni (see page 71)
Freshly grated kefalotyri or Parmesan
cheese, for accompaniment

Place chicken pieces in a glass or ceramic bowl. Sprinkle with lemon juice, ground cinnamon, salt, and pepper. Add cinnamon sticks and garlic; turn chicken pieces in mixture to coat evenly. Cover and refrigerate 2 hours.

Dilute tomato paste with the water. In a dutch oven or deep saucepan over medium-low heat, combine diluted tomato paste, tomatoes, and bay leaf. Bring to a simmer.

In a large skillet over medium-high heat, warm oil. Remove chicken from marinade and reserve marinade. Add onion and chicken to skillet and brown chicken on all sides. As each piece is browned, add it to the simmering tomato sauce. Then add browned onion, reserved marinade, and sherry to tomato sauce; bring slowly to a boil.

Add water, if needed, to cover chicken completely. Cover, reduce heat to very low, and simmer until chicken is tender (about 40 minutes).

Meanwhile, prepare macaroni, timing it so that it is ready when the chicken is done. Spoon some of the tomato sauce from the chicken over the macaroni. Remove chicken from sauce and arrange on a warmed platter. Serve macaroni, remaining tomato sauce, and the grated cheese in separate bowls alongside.

Serves 4

Chicken with Homemade Noodles
Kota me Spitisies Hilopites

*I*f you haven't the time to make the noodles, use one pound of commercial macaroni instead. Cook the macaroni in the same manner as the fresh noodles.

Homemade Noodles (see page 69)
2 frying chickens (about 3 lb each), cut
*   in serving pieces*
Salt and freshly ground pepper, to taste
¼ cup butter or olive oil
2 medium onions, chopped
1 clove garlic, minced
1 cup dry sherry
1 can (28 oz) plum tomatoes, coarsely
*   chopped, with their juice*
¼ teaspoon ground cinnamon
Freshly grated kefalotyri or Parmesan
*   cheese, for accompaniment*

Make noodle dough and cut noodles; cover with towel and set aside.

Season chicken pieces with salt and pepper. In a large skillet over medium-high heat, melt butter. Add chicken and brown lightly on all sides. Add onions and garlic and sauté until onions are translucent (about 5 minutes). Mix in sherry and tomatoes and bring to a slow boil. Cover, reduce heat to very low, and simmer until chicken is tender (about 40 minutes).

Meanwhile, bring a large pot of water to a boil. Add salt to taste and noodles; boil until noodles are half-cooked. Drain.

Remove chicken from sauce and arrange on a warmed platter; keep warm. Add noodles to sauce and simmer until tender. Remove from heat and sprinkle with cinnamon. Cover and let stand 5 minutes.

Transfer noodles to a serving bowl and serve with chicken. Pass a bowl of cheese.

Serves 6 to 8

Chicken with Yogurt

Kota me Yiaourti

*B*y the fifth century B.C. many Greeks were raising chickens. A few centuries later, farmers on the island of Cos perfected the fattening of birds for the table. The creation of this recipe couldn't have been far behind.

> *2 frying chickens, cut in serving pieces*
> *Juice of 1 lemon*
> *Salt and freshly ground pepper, to taste*
> *Butter, for sautéing*
> *1 onion, chopped*
> *1 clove garlic, minced*
> *½ cup dry white wine*
> *2 cups chicken stock*
> *Dash freshly grated nutmeg*
> *2 cups plain yogurt*
> *2 tablespoons flour*
> *3 tablespoons water*
> *Lemon wedges, for accompaniment*

Rub chicken pieces with lemon juice, salt, and pepper. In a large skillet over medium-high heat, melt butter. Add chicken, onion, and garlic; sauté chicken until lightly browned on all sides (6 to 8 minutes). Rapidly move pan back and forth over burner while slowly pouring in wine and 1 cup of the stock. Sprinkle in nutmeg. Reduce heat and cook, uncovered, until chicken is almost tender (about 25 minutes).

Meanwhile, place yogurt in a small saucepan over low heat. Dissolve flour in the water and slowly add mixture to yogurt, blending well. Gradually stir in the remaining stock and heat until well blended.

Add yogurt mixture to chicken and cook over very low heat, rapidly moving pan back and forth over burner, until sauce thickens.

Remove chicken from sauce and arrange on a warmed platter. Spoon sauce over chicken. Surround with lemon wedges and serve hot.

Serves 6

Chicken Stew with Okra
Kota Yahni me Bamyes

*H*ere is a versatile recipe—simply replace the okra with what looks best at the produce market or what is ready to harvest in your backyard garden.

1 frying chicken (about 4 lb), cut in
*   serving pieces*
Salt and freshly ground pepper, to taste
Olive oil or butter, for sautéing
1 large onion, chopped
1 clove garlic, minced
Minced fresh oregano, to taste
1 cup dry white wine
5 or 6 ripe tomatoes, peeled and
*   chopped, or 1 can (28 oz) plum*
*   tomatoes, chopped, with their liquid*
2 cups chicken stock
1 pound okra
Juice of ½ lemon

Sprinkle chicken pieces with salt and pepper. In a dutch oven over medium-high heat, heat olive oil. Add chicken pieces, onion, and garlic; sauté until chicken pieces are lightly browned on all sides (6 to 8 minutes). Sprinkle with oregano, then add wine, tomatoes, and stock. Cover, reduce heat to low, and simmer until chicken is tender (about 40 minutes).

Meanwhile, trim and discard stems from okra; be careful not to pierce pods. Place okra in a bowl and sprinkle lemon juice over top. Toss to mix. Twenty minutes before chicken is done, gently stir okra into chicken and tomatoes. Cook until tender.

Serves 4

Chicken Stew With Artichokes
(Kota Yahni me Anginares)

Omit okra. Remove 3 or 4 outer layers of leaves from 4 small artichokes. Slice 1 inch off tops and trim stems. Cut artichokes in half lengthwise and scoop out thistles with a spoon. Rub artichokes with juice of 1 lemon. Add to stew with stock.

Chicken Stew With Potatoes
(Kota Yahni me Patates)

Omit okra and lemon juice. Preheat oven to 350° F. Peel 8 small new potatoes. Prepare stew up to the point where stock is added, but do not simmer. Transfer chicken pieces to roasting pan; arrange potatoes around chicken and sprinkle with more minced fresh oregano. Spoon tomato sauce from dutch oven over chicken. Roast chicken and potatoes until tender (45 minutes to 1 hour).

Chicken Stew With Peas
(Kota Yahni me Bizelia)

Omit okra and lemon juice. Add 2 cups shelled peas (about 2 pounds unshelled) to stew 10 minutes before chicken is done.

HESTIA AND THE SAUCES OF GREECE

GGGGGGGGGGGGGGGGGGGGGGGGGGGGGGGGGGGGGGGGGGGGGGGGGGGGGGGGGGGGGGGGGGGGG

Hestia, Keeper of the Hearth

Hestia, wherever homes shelter,
raised to the sky,
men going on earth or gods
who many never die,
the foremost honour you've gained,
and a lasting place.
Noble your portion and right.
For, lacking your grace,
no mortal would dare to eat.
First, he must bend,
pouring sweet wine to you,
and again at the end.

Sauces give Greek cuisine much of its distinction and flavor. Fried or boiled vegetables and grilled seafood are transformed by a dollop of garlic sauce; the flavors of meat and fowl are deepened by simmering in a cinnamon-spiked tomato sauce. White sauce is a must in such tempting casseroles as pastitsio. And salads and boiled vegetables bathed in a dressing of olive oil and vinegar act as a refreshing foil for the richness of many Greek dishes.

Cheeses are also an indispensable part of the Greek pantry. They are baked with shrimp, strewn over freshly cooked macaroni, or fried until golden and buttery. Feta, the best-known Greek cheese, has been made in essentially the same manner—the milk is first curdled by lactic fermentation, then the curds are salted in brine—for thousands of years. Undoubtedly the gods dined on feta.

Tissue-thin filo dough is another important ingredient in Greek cuisine. Basted liberally with butter and baked, it makes a delicate wrapper for sweet and savory dishes. Filo preparations can be time-consuming but with some basic rules on handling, they need not be difficult.

Sauces, Dressings, and Yogurt

Many of the world's most famous sauces have their origin in Greek cookery. The classic white sauce, created two millenia ago by Orion, is the direct ancestor of the French béchamel. The brown sauce that was the work of Orion's compatriot, Lampriadas, is the ancient counterpart to the contemporary stock-and-vegetable mixtures that dress roasted meats and fowl.

Skordalia can be described as a mayonnaise of substance, laced with enough garlic to topple the Acropolis. Yet it can also be mellowed to suit the most sensitive palate. Might it not be the forerunner of the French aioli?

The most magnificent of all our contributions to the lexicon of sauces is *saltsa avgolemono*, which is used in soups and stews and as a topping for vegetables. It too was known in ancient times, for there are references to "sour sauce" in the writings of the day.

The Greeks began making yogurt thousands of years ago; they recognized it as both a healthful food and an excellent means of preserving milk. Modern Greeks eat *yiaourti* alone or with fruit, and use it in sauces to accompany meats and fowl.

Olive oil and vinegar were also standard pantry items in ancient times. Today they add a wonderful fragrance and flavor to raw and cooked vegetables, and can be mixed with tangy feta cheese in a piquant salad dressing.

Egg-Lemon Sauce

Saltsa Avgolemono

This most revered of all Greek sauces is used in many ways: spooned over vegetables, fish, and meats, or mixed into soups or braised dishes. If the sauce is going to be added to a soup or braised dish, omit the cornstarch.

1 cup stock
3 eggs
Juice of 2 lemons
1 tablespoon cornstarch
2 tablespoons water

Pour stock into a saucepan and bring to a simmer.

Select 1 medium mixing bowl and 1 small one. Break eggs, separating whites into larger bowl and yolks into smaller one. Beat whites until stiff peaks form. Whisk together yolks until blended, then slowly beat them into whites. Gradually add lemon juice to eggs, beating continuously.

Dissolve cornstarch in the water. Slowly add to simmering stock, stirring until well blended and stock thickens slightly. Gradually add stock to egg mixture, whisking continuously until smooth and creamy. Serve immediately.

Makes about 2 cups

Basic White Sauce

Aspri Saltsa

White sauce is used to bind two of our most renowned dishes, *moussaka* and *pastitsio*, but it is used in dozens of other ways as well.

2 cups milk
¼ cup butter
3 tablespoons flour
Salt and white pepper, to taste

Pour milk into a small, heavy-bottomed saucepan and bring to a boil; remove from heat. In a second heavy-bottomed saucepan over medium heat, melt butter. Add flour and cook, stirring, until well blended and bubbly (about 3 minutes); do not allow mixture to color.

Reduce heat to medium-low and gradually add hot milk, stirring continuously. Season with salt and pepper and increase heat; cook, stirring often, until slightly thickened (about 5 minutes). Adjust seasoning.

Makes about 2 cups

Basic White Sauce for Fish Substitute fish stock or bottled clam juice for half of the milk; season with juice of 1 lemon.

Basic White Sauce for Fowl Substitute chicken stock for half of the milk. Season with a dash of ground cinnamon, a dash of brandy, and 1 teaspoon freshly grated orange zest.

Basic White Sauce for Vegetables Substitute chicken stock for half of the milk. Add juice of 1 lemon, a dash of crushed dried thyme, and ½ cup grated cheese of choice.

White Sauce with Raisins

Aspri Saltsa me Stafedes

GGGGGGGGGGGGGGGGGGGGGGGGGGGGGGGGGGGGGGGGGGGGGGGGGGGGGGGGGGGGGGGGGGGGGGGGGGGG

*R*aisins and sherry turn a simple white sauce into an elegant topping for broiled fish or poultry.

½ cup raisins
1 cup dry sherry
½ recipe Basic White Sauce (see page 174)
Dash each freshly grated nutmeg and
   ground cinnamon
1 tablespoon freshly squeezed lemon
   juice

In a small bowl combine raisins and sherry; set aside.

Prepare white sauce and add raisins and sherry, nutmeg, cinnamon, and lemon juice; simmer over medium heat, stirring often, until flavors are well blended (15 minutes).

Makes about 2 cups

Grape Sauce

Saltsa Stafelia

GGGGGGGGGGGGGGGGGGGGGGGGGGGGGGGGGGGGGGGGGGGGGGGGGGGGGGGGGGGGGGGGGGGGGGGGGGGG

*U*se small Thompson seedless grapes for this sauce. Serve with roast game birds or chicken; using the pan juices from the roasting birds to flavor the sauce.

½ recipe Basic White Sauce (see page 174)
1 cup small seedless grapes
2 tablespoons brandy, or to taste
½ cup defatted pan juices, from roasting
   poultry, or stock
Salt and freshly ground pepper, to taste
Butter (optional)

Prepare white sauce and add grapes, brandy, and pan juices; simmer over medium heat, stirring, until well blended and grapes are heated through (3 to 5 minutes).

Adjust seasoning with salt, pepper, and brandy. For a richer sauce, stir in butter to taste.

Makes about 2 cups

Garlic Sauce
Skordalia

As an accompaniment to seafood, this sauce has no peer. It may be served with hot or cold halibut, fresh cod, salt cod, lobster, or shrimp. You can even dilute it with some bottled clam juice or fish stock to make a thinner sauce. It is also an excellent complement to vegetables: chilled artichoke halves; fried zucchini, eggplant, or cauliflower; or boiled spinach or Swiss chard. To prepare canapés, spread the sauce on toasted bread triangles or squares and top with a tiny cooked shrimp or lobster chunk. As your addiction to this marvelously aromatic sauce grows, you will discover a variety of new uses for it.

6 cloves garlic, cut up
2 cups mashed cooked potatoes
½ teaspoon salt
1 cup olive oil
½ cup white wine vinegar

In a food processor or blender, process garlic briefly to mince. Add potatoes and salt and process at high speed until smooth. Alternating oil with vinegar, slowly add liquids in a fine, steady stream. Blend until smooth, thick, and creamy. If sauce is too thick, thin with a little water.

Makes about 3 cups

Garlic Sauce With Nuts In a blender pulverize 1 cup chopped walnuts or blanched almonds. Mix into Garlic Sauce.

Garlic Sauce Dip Combine ½ cup Garlic Sauce, 1 cup plain yogurt, and 1 teaspoon almond extract. Mix thoroughly, chill, and serve with an assortment of crackers.

Garlic Sauce Evoula

Skordalia à la Evoul

GGGGGGGGGGGGGGGGGGGGGGGGGGGGGGGGGGGGG

*T*his is my own creation. It is more delicately flavored and easier to prepare than traditional garlic sauce.

3 small cloves garlic
1 cup mashed cooked potatoes
½ cup mayonnaise
1 tablespoon olive oil

In a food processor or blender, process garlic briefly to mince. Add potatoes, mayonnaise, and oil. Process until smooth and creamy.

Makes about 2 cups

Quick Tomato Sauce

Saltsa Domata

GGGGGGGGGGGGGGGGGGGGGGGGGGGGGGGGGGGGGGG

*T*his fragrant tomato sauce can be served over macaroni or combined with fresh green beans, peas, or other raw vegetables in a saucepan and cooked until vegetables are tender. Or, try it spooned over fried fish, roasted chicken, or an omelet.

6 tablespoons butter or olive oil
6 green onions (including some green
*   top), chopped*
2 cloves garlic, minced
¼ cup chopped fresh parsley
6 ripe tomatoes, peeled and chopped, or
*   1 can (28 oz) tomatoes, chopped, with*
*   their liquid*
1 tablespoon each minced fresh oregano
*   and mint*
2 bay leaves
½ cup dry sherry
Salt and freshly ground pepper, to taste

In a large skillet over medium-high heat, melt butter. Add onions, garlic, and parsley; sauté until onions are translucent (about 5 minutes). Stir in tomatoes, mixing well. Add oregano, mint, bay leaves, and sherry.

Simmer, uncovered, over medium-high heat until mixture is thick (15 to 20 minutes). Discard bay leaves and season with salt and pepper.

Makes about 2 cups

Basic Tomato Sauce
Saltsa Domata

This sauce has an intense flavor and smooth, thick texture. Use it instead of canned tomato sauce whenever possible.

½ cup olive oil
1 medium onion, chopped
2 cloves garlic, minced
3 pounds ripe tomatoes, peeled, seeded,
  and chopped, or 2 cans (16 oz each)
  plum tomatoes, chopped, with their
  liquid
2 tablespoons minced fresh oregano or
  ½ tablespoon dried oregano, crushed
2 bay leaves
Salt and freshly ground pepper, to taste

In a large skillet over medium-high heat, warm oil. Add onion and garlic and sauté until translucent (about 5 minutes). Add tomatoes, oregano, and bay leaves; stir well.

Simmer, uncovered, over low heat until sauce is thick (about 1 hour). Stir occasionally to prevent sticking. Discard bay leaves and season to taste with salt and pepper. Force through a sieve to create a smooth consistency. Cool, cover, and store in refrigerator up to 1 week.

Makes about 3 cups

Yogurt Sauce
Saltsa Yiaourt

Spoon this sauce over grilled or roasted lamb or chicken. Use stock or pan juices that complement the meat.

2 tablespoons flour
2 tablespoons water
1 cup plain yogurt
½ cup each dry white wine and stock or
  pan juices
Salt and white pepper, to taste

Dissolve flour in the water. In a heavy-bottomed saucepan over low heat, gently heat yogurt. Mix in flour mixture, then slowly pour in wine, stirring constantly.

Simmer, uncovered, over very low heat 15 minutes. Add stock, blend well, and season with salt and pepper. Serve at once.

Makes about 2 cups

Savory Sauce for Fish

Saltsa Savori

ᴳᴳᴳᴳᴳᴳᴳᴳᴳᴳᴳᴳᴳᴳᴳᴳᴳᴳᴳᴳᴳᴳᴳᴳᴳᴳᴳᴳᴳᴳᴳᴳᴳᴳᴳᴳᴳᴳᴳ

*T*his sauce will keep in the refrigerator for a few days. Reheat gently and serve over panfried fish steaks or fillets.

1 cup olive oil
2 tablespoons flour
1 cup water
½ cup white wine vinegar
½ cup Basic Tomato Sauce (see page 178)
4 cloves garlic, blanched 1 minute,
*   drained, and slivered*
3 bay leaves
Salt and freshly ground pepper, to taste
1 tablespoon chopped fresh rosemary
1 teaspoon ground allspice

In a skillet over medium heat, warm oil. Dissolve flour in the water and gradually add to saucepan, stirring until smooth. Add vinegar, tomato sauce, garlic, bay leaves, salt, and pepper. Simmer, stirring occasionally, 20 minutes.

Add rosemary and allspice, stir well, and remove from heat. Serve at once or cool, cover, and store in refrigerator.

Makes about 2 cups

Basic Marinade for Grilled Meats and Fish

Saltsa Marinata

ᴳᴳᴳᴳᴳᴳᴳᴳᴳᴳᴳᴳᴳᴳᴳᴳᴳᴳᴳᴳᴳᴳᴳᴳᴳᴳᴳᴳᴳᴳᴳᴳᴳᴳᴳᴳᴳᴳᴳ

*M*atch the wine in this marinade to the meat: red wine for red meats and game and white wine for fish and poultry.

Marinate fish 1 to 2 hours; marinate poultry and meat as long as overnight, depending upon the desired intensity of flavor. Be sure to cover and refrigerate mixture if marinating longer than 1 hour.

Before grilling bring meats or fish to room temperature; baste with marinade as they cook.

2 cups wine
1 cup olive oil
2 cloves garlic, crushed
1 tablespoon minced fresh oregano
2 bay leaves
Juice of 2 lemons
¼ cup chopped fresh parsley

In a glass or ceramic vessel, combine all ingredients and mix well.

Makes about 3 ¹/₄ cups

Feta Dressing Evoula

Saltsa Feta

GGGGGGGGGGGGGGGGGGGGGGGGGGGGGGGGGG

I created this quick-and-easy dressing for tossing with any green salad. The Worcestershire sauce makes it a truly Greek-American creation.

2 cloves garlic
2 cups crumbled feta cheese
2 cups mayonnaise
½ cup red wine vinegar
1 teaspoon dried fines herbs, crushed
1 tablespoon minced fresh oregano
1 tablespoon Worcestershire sauce
2 tablespoons olive oil

In a food processor or blender, process garlic to mince. Add remaining ingredients and blend until smooth. Store in a covered jar in refrigerator for up to 10 days.

Makes about 4 cups

Variation If a coarser dressing is desired, mince garlic, combine all ingredients in a jar, cap tightly, and shake well to mix.

Basic Vinaigrette

Saltsa Ladoxeidou

GGGGGGGGGGGGGGGGGGGGGGGGGGGGGGGGGG

U se this classic oil-and-vinegar dressing on tossed salads or cold cooked vegetables.

⅔ cup olive oil, or to taste
⅓ cup wine vinegar, or to taste
Salt and freshly ground pepper, to taste
Minced fresh or crushed dried oregano
*   or other herb, to taste (optional)*

In a small bowl combine oil and vinegar. Whisk to blend and season with salt and pepper. Adjust seasoning, adding more oil or vinegar to taste. Add herb (if used).

Makes about 1 cup

Homemade Mayonnaise
Mayoneza

ᎶᎶᎶᎶᎶᎶᎶᎶᎶᎶᎶᎶᎶᎶᎶᎶᎶᎶᎶᎶᎶᎶᎶᎶᎶᎶᎶᎶᎶᎶᎶ

Greeks love to eat cold poached seafood with creamy homemade mayonnaise. You can also use this mayonnaise as a base for a creamy salad dressing.

2 egg yolks
Pinch each salt and white pepper, or to
taste
2 tablespoons freshly squeezed lemon
juice
1 cup olive oil

In a food processor or blender, whirl egg yolks, salt, white pepper, lemon juice and ¼ cup of the oil until well blended.

With machine running, pour in the remaining oil in a fine, steady stream. Process briefly until thick. Adjust seasoning.

Makes about 1 ¼ cups

Homemade Yogurt
Yiaourti

ᎶᎶᎶᎶᎶᎶᎶᎶᎶᎶᎶᎶᎶᎶᎶᎶᎶᎶᎶᎶᎶᎶᎶᎶᎶᎶᎶᎶᎶᎶᎶᎶᎶᎶ

Yogurt is so healthy, popular, and versatile, why not make your own? This simple method is fool-proof. The yogurt can be stored in the refrigerator for up to 4 days.

4 cups milk
½ cup whipping cream
2 tablespoons plain yogurt

In a saucepan over medium-low heat, combine milk and cream and bring slowly to a boil. Stir constantly to prevent mixture from scorching. Simmer 10 minutes. Remove from heat and cool slightly.

Dilute yogurt in a little of the milk and stir it into the rest of the milk. Mix well and pour into small jars. Cover and let stand in a warm place overnight. When yogurt is set, refrigerate.

Makes about 1 quart

MENUS FOR SPECIAL OCCASIONS

*F*estive meals are an integral part of Greek life. Whether the occasion is a religious holiday or just a gathering of friends, a bounteous supper is the centerpiece of the event. Plan your own celebrations, Greek style, with these four special menus.

"I loved thee, Attis, long ago,"
said Sappho of Lesbos, the tenth muse.
Who in all truth would inspire
a supper for lovers,
or lovers to be,
but Sappho, our love poetess?
Tragic,
torn between lesbianism and love of
man.
Woman prevailed,
and as the tale goes,
Sappho flung herself into the sea,
for the love of a man!
Here is a supper for lovers,
married or single,
love is love,
and lovers are lovers.

Sappho:
A Lovers' Supper
for Two

Mavrodaphne over crushed ice

*Half recipe Chilled Chicken and
Egg-Lemon Soup
(see page 33)*

*Half recipe Stuffed Squabs in Foil
(see page 162)*

*Broiled Tomatoes with Feta
(see page 20)*

Chilled white retsina

Fresh fruit

Coffee and Metaxa brandy

Terpischore: After the Ballet, A Buffet for Eight

Ouzo on the rocks

Pâté à la Grecque
(see page 27)

Kalamata olives

Kasseri cheese

Double recipe Shoulder of Lamb
Stuffed with Eggplant
(see page 120)

Sliced cucumbers and tomatoes
drizzled with Feta Dressing Evoula
(see page 180)

Crusty bread

Chilled white retsina

Clove Cookies
(see page 84)

Metaxa brandy

Of all the muses,
none is so graceful as Terpsichore.
To set the pace of an evening,
evoke Terpsichore,
dim the lights,
and laden your table with godly bits.
The spirit of the goddess of the dance is
among you.
The prelude is yours.
The twilight of the gods is postponed.
Feast and dance.

*The audaciously beautiful, flight-bound
figure of Nike of Samothrace
is the symbol of Greece's freedom.
She seems to be arrested by eternity
as she keeps vigil,
for those who slumber, for freedom.
The Greeks commemorate their freedom
from the Turks every spring.
Throughout the world, on March 25,
a pageant appears in the name of
Victory.*

*Nike:
The Victory Buffet
for Twelve*

Mavrodaphne over crushed ice

*Eggplant Dip
(see page 42)*

*Spinach-Cheese Triangles
(see page 19)*

*Rice-Stuffed Squid
(see page 26)*

*Stuffed Grape Leaves
(see page16)*

Sliced tomatoes and feta cheese

*Double recipe Shrimp Pilaf
(see page 104)*

*Assorted Vegetable Fritters
(see page 63)*

*Garlic Sauce
(see page 176)*

Chilled white retsina

*Custard with Filo
(see page75)*

The Greek Easter Feast for Eight

Fish Roe Purée
(see page 22)

Assorted Greek cheeses

Easter Soup
(see page 37)

Athenian Salad
(see page 41)

Kid on a Spit
(see page 117)

Potatoes Browned in Butter, Oven Variation
(see page 60)

Spinach-Cheese Pie
(see page 49)

Easter Bread
(see page 89)

Chilled white retsina

Sesame-Topped Butter Cookies
(see page 85)

Nut-and-Honey-Filled Filo Pastry
(see page 81)

Farina Diamonds
(see page 79)

Coffee and Metaxa brandy

Greek Easter is a panorama of great pageantry.
A profound and revered respect
is paid to our Lord by Greeks throughout the world.
Whether it be in a remote Greek village,
or the streets of Athens, or the cities of America.
At the resurrection services on Easter eve,
a unity of voices chants "Christos Anesti,"
"Christ has risen,"
making a god of every Greek.
Easter Sunday is complete abandonment.
The fasting is over. The feast is on.

INDEX

APPETIZERS

Angouria Yemista me Feta, 20
Cheese, Fried, 19
Cocktail Meatballs, 28
Cucumbers Stuffed with Feta, 20
Domates me Feta, 20
Dolmadakia, 16
Feta Cheese Triangles, 17
Fish Roe Purée, 22
Garides à la Plaka, 24
Grape Leaves, Stuffed, 16
Kalamaria Toursi, 25
Kalamaria Yemista, 26
Kasseri Tiganismeno, 19
Keftaidakia, 28
Kreatopetes, 18
Lamb Brains Marinated with
    Oregano, 29
Liver Bits, Fried, 28
Manitaria Marinata, 21
Marides Tighanites, 23
Meat Triangles, 18
Miala Riganata, 29
Mushrooms, Marinated, 21
Pâté à la Grecque, 27
Psaropetes, 18
Shellfish Triangles, 18
Shrimp in Their Shells, Plaka Style, 24
Sikotakia Tighanita, 28
Spanakopetes, 19
Spinach-Cheese Triangles, 19
Squid, Pickled, 25
Squid, Rice-Stuffed, 26
Taramosalata, 22
Tiropetes, 17
Tomatoes with Feta, Broiled, 20
Whitebait, Fried, 23

SOUPS

Bean with Vegetables, 38
Celery and Egg-Lemon, 33
Chicken and Egg-Lemon, 33
Chicken and Egg-Lemon, Chilled, 34
Easter, 37
Fassoulada, 38
Lentil, 39
Mageritsa, 37
Meatballs and Egg-Lemon, 35
Skembe Soupa, 36
Soupa
    Avgolemono, 33
    Faki, 39
    Krya Avgolemono, 34
    Selino Avgolemono, 33
    Trahana, 39
Tripe and Egg-Lemon, 36
Trahana, 39
Youvarlakia, 35

SALADS

Angourosalata me Yiaourti, 43
Athenian Salad, 41
Avocado me Taramosalata, 45
Avocado with Fish Roe Purée, 45
Beet and Onion, 45
Cabbage, 46
Cucumbers with Yogurt, 43
Domatosalata me Feta, 42
Domatosalata me Sardeles, 43
Eggplant Salad or Dip, 42
Hot Potato Salad, 46
Kokinogoulia Salata, 45
Lahano Salata, 46
Melitzanosalata, 42
Psari Salata me Mayoneza, 44
Salata Athenas, 41
Seafood Salad with Mayonnaise, 44
Tomatoes with Anchovies and
    Capers, 43
Tomatoes with Feta Dressing, 42
Zesti Patatosalata, 46

VEGETABLE ENTRÉES AND SIDE DISHES

Anginares Pilafi, 57
Apples Stuffed with Raisins and Nuts,
    54
Artichoke Omelet, 54
Artichokes and Rice, 57
Avga
    me Anginares, 54
    me Domates, 55
    me Kolokithaki, 55
Bamyes Yahni, 59
Cabbage, Stuffed, 53
Carrots Sautéed in Butter, 59
Cauliflower Fritters with Garlic
    Sauce, 63

Celery Hearts in Egg-Lemon Sauce, 61
Domates Yemistes, 52
Domates Yemistes me Rizi, 52
Eggplant with Lamb, Baked, 48
Greens Sauté, Mixed, 60
Greens with Lemon Juice and Olive Oil, Boiled, 61
Horta Tighanita, 60
Horta Vrasta, 61
Karota Tighanita, 59
Kolokithia Tighanita, 62
Krokettes Skordalia, 63
Lahanika me Aspri Saltsa, 65
Lahanika me Saltsa Domata, 64
Lahanodolmades, 53
Lima Bean Plaki, 58
Lopia Plaki, 58
Mila Yemistes, 54
Mixed Greens Sauté, 60
Mixed Vegetable Casserole, 56
Moussaka, 48
Okra Braised with Tomatoes, 59
Papoutsakia, 50
Patates Tighanites, 60
Potatoes Browned in Butter, 60
Selino Avgolemono, 61
Spinach-Cheese Pie, 49
Spanakopeta, 49
Spanakorizo, 56
Spinach and Rice, 56
Tomatoes
  and Eggs, 55
  Stuffed with Beef and Zucchini, 51
  Stuffed with Rice, 52
Vegetable Casserole, Mixed, 56
Vegetables with Tomato Sauce, 64
Vegetables with White Sauce, 65

Zucchini
  and Eggs, 55
  Fried in Olive Oil, 62
  Stuffed, 50

RICE AND NOODLES

Athenian Macaroni, 71
Beef and Macaroni Casserole, 70
Macaroni with Meat Sauce, 72
Makaronada, 71
Makaronia Kima, 72
Noodles, Homemade, 69
Rice
  and Fides Pilaf, 66
  Pilaf, 67
  Pilaf with Mushrooms, 68
  with Tomato Sauce, 67
Pastitsio, 70
Pilafi, 67
Pilafi me Fides, 66
Pilafi me Manitaria, 68
Rizi Yahni, 67
Spitisies Hilopite, 69

SWEETS AND BREADS

Custards, Puddings, and Confections
Athenian Rice Pudding, 76
Baked Halvah, 77
Custard with Filo, 75
Custard Filo Rolls, 75
Farina Diamonds, 79
Galatoboureko, 75
Galatopeta, 74
Grape Must Pudding, 76
Halvah, 79
Halvah tou Fournou, 77

Moustoalevria, 76
Orange-Almond Crêpes, 78
Orange-Scented Custard, 74
Rizogalo, 76
Tighanites Yemistes, 78

Pastries, Cakes, and Cookies
Baklava, 81
Clove Cookies, 84
Diples, 82
Honey Puffs, 83
Honey Rolls, 82
Karidopeta, 80
Koulourakia, 85
Kourabiedes, 84
Loukoumades, 83
Nut-and-Honey-Filled Filo Pastry, 81
Sesame-Topped Butter Cookies, 85
Walnut Cake, 80

Spoon Sweets
Cytro Glyko, 87
Grapefruit Spoon Sweet, 87
Kythoni me Amygthala Glyko, 88
Orange Spoon Sweet, 87
Portokali Glyko, 87
Quince-Almond Spoon Sweet, 88
Rose-Petal Spoon Sweet, 88
Triantafillo Glyko, 88

Breads
Easter Bread, 89
Easter Twists, 90
Lambropsomo, 89
New Year's Bread, 91
Tsoureki, 90
Vasilopeta, 91

FISH AND SHRIMP

Avga me Psariou, 106
Bakaliaros me Spanaki, 101
Bakaliaros Plaki, 101
Cod, Fresh, Baked with Currants, 101
Cod, Fresh, with Spinach and Garlic Sauce, 101
Fish
  Baked with Tomatoes, 99
  Kalamata Style, Baked, 95
  Soup, 96
Garides
  me Feta, 103
  Pilafi, 104
  Souvlakia, 105
Halibut with Shrimp Sauce, 102
Pompano, Baked, 99
Psari
  Fournou à la Kalamai, 95
  me Saltsa Garides, 102
  me Saltsa Stafedes, 100
  Plaki, 99
  Psito, 99
  sto Harti, 100
  Yemisto, 98
Psarosoupa, 96
Seafood Omelet, 106
Shrimp
  on Skewers, 105
  Pilaf, 104
  with Feta in Casserole, 103
Sole with Raisin Sauce, 100
Striped Sea Bass, with Currant-Rice Stuffing, 98
Trout in Foil, 100

SALT COD, OCTOPUS, SQUID, AND EEL

Bakaliaros
  Kefte Skordalia, 107
  me Aspri Saltsa, 108
  tou Fournou, 109
Cheli
  me Domates, 113
  Tighanito, 114
  tis Skaras, 112
Eel
  Broiled, 112
  Fried, 114
  in Tomato Sauce, 113
Kalamaria Yemista, 112
Octopus in Wine, 111
Octopus Pilaf, 110
Oktapodi Krassato, 111
Oktapodi Pilafi, 110
Salt Cod
  in Casserole with White Sauce, 108
  Patties with Garlic Sauce, 107
  with Tomato Sauce, Baked, 109
Stuffed Squid, 112

KID AND LAMB

Arnaki Yemisto, 121
Arni
  à la Pallakari, 119
  Giouvetsi, 129
  Kapama, 130
  Kleftiko, 128
  me Anginares, 125
  me Yiaourti, 124
  Psito, 118
  Souvlakia, 122
  sto Harti, 127
Yahni, 130
Yemisto me Melitzana, 120
Avga me Nafra, 132
Cephalonian Meat Pie, 123
Glossa Arniou Ladoxeidou, 134
Glossa Arniou me Saltsa, 135
Katsikaki tis Souvlas, 117
Kid on a Spit, 117
Kreatopita, 123
Lamb
  Bandit Style, 128
  Brains Baked with Eggs, 136
  Brains, Fried, 137
  Brains in White Sauce, 137
  Broth and Shanks, 118
  in Tomato Sauce with Macaroni, 130
  Kidney Omelet, 132
  Kidney Pilaf, 134
  Kidneys on Skewers, 133
  Shoulder Stuffed with Eggplant, 120
  Leg of, in Foil, 119
  on Skewers, 122
  Roast Leg of, 118
  Shanks, Baked, 126
  Shanks in Foil, 127
  Steaks and Artichokes, Baked, 125
  Stew, 131
  Stuffed Crown, 121
  Tongues in Sauce, 135
  Tongues Vinaigrette, 134
  with Kritharaki, 129
  with Yogurt, 124
Miala
  me Aspri Saltsa, 137
  sto Fournou, 136
  Tighanita, 137
Nafra Pilafi, 134

Nafra Souvlakia, 133
Podarakia Arniou, 126
Zomos Arniou, 118

Pheasant Stuffed with Grapes, 152
Rabbit in Foil, 154
Venison Steaks with Tomato Sauce, 155

Sunday Chicken Dinner, 166
Turkey with Chestnut Stuffing, Roast, 156

VEAL, BEEF, AND PORK

Beef Stew with Onions, 140
Beef with Vegetables, Boiled, 130
Calves' Liver with Oregano, 142
Gourounopoulo Psito, 145
Hirino me Selino Avgolemono, 147
Keftaides, 143
Meat Roll Stuffed with Eggs, 141
Meatballs with Mint, 143
Mosharaki me Anginares, 139
Mosharaki me Aspri Saltsa, 138
Pig, Roast Suckling, 146
Pork and Celery with Egg-Lemon Sauce, 147
Rolo, 141
Sikotaki Riganato, 145
Skembe me Salt, 145
Souzoukakia, 144
Stefado, 140
Tripe Sauté, 145
Veal Birds with Artichokes Evoula, 139
Veal Chops with White Sauce, 138
Vothino Vrasto, 130

GAME BIRDS, RABBIT, AND VENISON

Elafi me Saltsa Domata, 155
Fasianos Yemistos, 152
Game Birds with Wild Rice Stuffing, Roast, 151
Kotopoulo Kyniyo Yemisto, 151
Lagos Kleftiko, 154

TURKEY, GOOSE, DUCK, SQUAB, AND CHICKEN

Chena Yemiste, 158
Chicken
    Artichoke-Stuffed, in Foil, 163
    Breasts with Pine-Nut Rice, 165
    in Tomato Sauce with Macaroni, 167
    Roast Stuffed, Plaka Style, 164
    Stew with Okra, 170
    Sunday Dinner, 166
    with Homemade Noodles, 168
    with Yogurt, 169
Duck in Wine with Potatoes, Roast, 159
Duck with Apple Stuffing, Roast, 160
Galopoulo Yemisto, 156
Goose with Chestnut-Apple Stuffing, Roast, 158
Kota
    Avgolemono, 166
    Kapama, 167
    me Koukounari, 165
    me Spitisies Hilopites, 168
    me Yiaourti, 169
    Yahni me Bamyes, 170
    Yemista à la Plaka, 164
    Yemista sto Harti, 163
Papaki Psito me Patates, 159
Papaki Yemisto, 160
Peristeri sto Harti, 162
Squabs in Foil, Stuffed, 162

SAUCES, DRESSINGS, AND YOGURT

Aspri Saltsa, 174
Aspri Saltsa me Stafedes, 175
Egg-Lemon Sauce, 173
Feta Dressing Evoula, 180
Garlic Sauce, 176
Garlic Sauce Evoula, 177
Grape Sauce, 176
Marinade for Grilled Meats and Fish, Basic, 179
Mayoneza, 181
Mayonnaise, Homemade, 181
Saltsa
    Avgolemono, 173
    Domata, 177, 178
    Feta, 180
    Ladoxeidou, 180
    Marinata, 179
    Savori, 179
    Stafelia, 176
    Yiaourt, 178
Savory Sauce for Fish, 179
Skordalia, 176
Skordalia à la Evoul, 177
Tomato Sauce, Basic, 178
Tomato Sauce, Quick, 177
Vinaigrette, Basic, 180
White Sauce, Basic, 174
White Sauce with Raisins, 175
Yiaourti, 181
Yogurt, Homemade, 181
Yogurt Sauce, 178

101 PRODUCTIONS COOKBOOKS

Softcover Titles

The Art of Cooking for Two by Coralie Castle & Astrid Newton	$9.95
Barbecue & Smoke Cookery by Maggie Waldron	$8.95
Bread & Breakfast by Linda Kay Bistrow	$10.95
The Calculating Cook by Jeanne Jones	$8.95
Coffee by Kenneth Davids	$10.95
The Ethnic Vegetarian by Shanta Nimbark Sacharoff	$8.95
Fifteen Minute Meals by Emalee Chapman	$8.95
Flavors of Hungary by Charlotte Slovak Biro	$10.95
Flavors of India by Shanta Nimbark Sacharoff	$8.95
Flavors of Japan by Delphine & Diane J. Hirasuna	$8.95
Flavors of Mexico by Angeles de la Rosa & C. Gandia de Fernández	$8.95
Flavors of Northern Italy by Violeta Autumn	$8.95
From Sea & Stream by Lou Seibert Pappas	$8.95
Greek Cooking for the Gods by Eva Zane	$10.95
Grill It In! by Barbara Grunes	$10.95
Home & Grill by Barbara Grunes	$10.95
Juice It Up! by Pat Gentry	$10.95
Kabobs on the Grill by Barbara Grunes	$10.95
Eggplant Mediterranee by Sotiris Kitrilakis	$11.95
The Hors d'Oeuvre Book by Coralie Castle	$10.95
Kitchen Tools by Patricia Gentry	$8.95
More Calculated Cooking by Jeanne Jones	$8.95
The New Harvest by Lou Seibert Pappas & Jane Horn	$9.95
One Pot Meals by Maggie Gin	$8.95
Pasta International by Gertrude Harris	$8.95
The Portable Feast by Diane D. MacMillan	$8.95
Real Bread by Maggie Baylis & Coralie Castle	$10.95
Secrets of Salt-Free Cooking by Jeanne Jones	$10.95
Some Like It Hotter by Geraldine Duncann	$10.95
Soup by Coralie Castle	$10.95
The Tea Lover's Treasury by James Norwood Pratt	$9.95
Vegetarian Gourmet Cookery by Alan Hooker	$10.95

Hardcover Titles

Diet for a Happy Heart by Jeanne Jones	$17.95
Teatime Celebrations by Patricia Gentry	$15.95

101 Productions and *California Culinary Academy* cookbooks are available from your local bookseller, or directly from The Cole Group, Inc., 4415 Sonoma Hwy., Santa Rosa, CA 95409. For a free catalog of all our cooking titles, call (707) 538-0495.

PRICES SUBJECT TO CHANGE WITHOUT NOTICE